W9-CTJ-034

THE
POWER OF
POSITIVE
NON<u>SE</u>NSE

BY LEO ROSTEN

O K*A*P*L*A*N! MY K*A*P*L*A*N!
THE 3:10 TO ANYWHERE
THE LOOK BOOK (ed.)
A NEW GUIDE AND ALMANAC TO THE
RELIGIONS OF AMERICA (ed.)
DEAR "HERM"
LEO ROSTEN'S TREASURY OF
JEWISH QUOTATIONS
ROME WASN'T BURNED IN A DAY: The Mischief
of Language
PEOPLE I HAVE LOVED, KNOWN OR ADMIRED
A TRUMPET FOR REASON
THE JOYS OF YIDDISH
A MOST PRIVATE INTRIGUE
THE MANY WORLDS OF LEO ROSTEN
CAPTAIN NEWMAN, M.D.
RELIGIONS IN AMERICA (ed.)
THE STORY BEHIND THE PAINTING
THE RETURN OF H*Y*M*A*N K*A*P*L*A*N
A GUIDE TO THE RELIGIONS OF AMERICA (ed.)
THE DARK CORNER
SLEEP, MY LOVE
112 GRIPES ABOUT THE FRENCH (War Department)
HOLLYWOOD: The Movie Colony, The Movie Makers
DATELINE: EUROPE
THE STRANGEST PLACES
THE WASHINGTON CORRESPONDENTS
THE EDUCATION OF H*Y*M*A*N K*A*P*L*A*N

THE POWER OF POSITIVE NONSENSE

Leo Rosten

McGraw-Hill Book Company

New York St. Louis San Francisco London
Mexico Sydney Toronto Düsseldorf

Book design by Marcy J. Katz.
Copyright © 1977 by Leo Rosten.
All rights reserved. Printed in the United States of America. No
part of this publication may be reproduced, stored in a retrieval
system, or transmitted, in any form or by any means, electronic,
mechanical, photocopying, recording, or otherwise, without the
prior written permission of the publisher.

1 2 3 4 5 6 7 8 9 0 BP BP 7 8 3 2 1 0 9 8 7

Library of Congress Cataloging in Publication Data

Rosten, Leo Calvin, date
The power of positive nonsense.
1 American wit and humor. I. Title.
PN6162.R66   818'.5'207   77-8067
ISBN 0-07-053985-5

To
the Kid from Kedzie

CONTENTS

"Aristotle calls man the rational animal. All my life I have been seeking evidence to confirm this."

Bertrand Russell

1.
POOR ROSTEN'S ALMANAC

"Everyone is ignorant, only
on different subjects."

—*Will Rogers*

I never stop marveling over the stuff people believe: the nonsense they accept without questioning, the twaddle they elevate to truisms, the drivel, twiddle, platitudes and flapdoodle they consider part of our storehouse of inherited wisdom. Not a day goes by without my hearing or reading flummery so fallacious but so familiar that it has been transformed, by time and repetition, into "obvious" pieces of "common sense," "self-evident" sayings whose truth "everyone knows."

Well, what everyone knows is often what no one has examined. I sometimes think that nothing on this befuddled globe is more widely spread, deeply rooted and gravely glorified than—baloney.

Suppose we cast a fresh eye on some sacred capsules of wisdom each of us learned at our first and dearest school: Mother's Knee. The results are unnerving. Even Ben Franklin's hallowed aphorisms often boil down to hollow hokum.

Take the phrase "idle curiosity." Every time I hear that, I get an acute attack of the glums. For surely, if you think about it for as long as ten seconds, you will

Poor Rosten's Almanac

agree that the one thing curiosity can *not* be is idle. (Yussel Umglick's *Principles of Logic* hailed this as "Rosten's First Law," but it happens to be my second. My first runs: "Don't blame God: He's only human.")

Now, if you'll fasten your mental seat belt, I'll take you on an antiseptic tour through 61 popular and beloved articles of faith which turn out to be bubblegum. Do not think me cynical: I am trying to be clinical.

1. "A picture is worth a thousand words."

Then why do you need words to make the point?
Better yet, draw me a picture of the Gettysburg Address.

2. "Two heads are better than one."

Not if both are stupid.
The only place I can think of where two heads are better than one is a Ringling Brothers sideshow. In other places, personnel interviewers are shamelessly prejudiced against a job applicant who sports two heads.

3. "Easy come, easy go."

This doesn't apply to houseguests.

4. "All power to the people!"

The people who holler "All power to the people!" want power to be handed over to the people who holler "All power to the people!"
Karl Marx did not understand this. Lenin did. So did Castro.

The Power of Positive Nonsense

5. "Give a man enough rope and he'll hang himself."

Don't be a fool: If you give a man enough rope he'll hang you.

6. "Rome wasn't built in a day."

It wasn't burned in a day, either.

7. "He's as honest as the day is long."

That's not much of a character reference. What does he do at night, rob delicatessens?

8. "Barking dogs don't bite."

I once patted a barking Chow on the head; he stopped barking and bit a hole in my wrist.

"Barking dogs don't read silly maxims" runs Rosten's 13th Law.

9. "Never put off until tomorrow what you can do today."

Including suicide?

My tuba teacher, Siegfried Krakauer, began to feel so guilty about his habit of putting things off, day after day, that he decided to end his disgusting indecisiveness once and for all. So he picked up the phone and briskly told his broker to sell ten thousand shares of Stretch-on Sausage Casings.

The next day S.S.C. bought out Xerox, declared a 30 percent dividend, and split the combined shares ten for one. Siegfried blew his brains out with a Colt .45, whose stock instantly jumped twelve points.

That's the sort of trouble you can get into if you take a stupid saying seriously.

10. "It's the exception that proves the rule."

Of all the idiotic illogic ever uttered, this one takes the cake. Is no rule proved until you can find an exception to it?

Take my advice and paste Rosten's 14th Law on your bathroom mirror: "The exception disproves the rule, for it proves that the rule isn't sound enough to cover all the cases to which it should apply." That's why Sherlock Holmes frostily told Dr. Watson, "I never make exceptions."

11. "Don't count your chickens until they're hatched."

Anyone who counts chickens before they're hatched is counting eggs, not chickens. Pay no attention to a dummy like that.

12. "Honesty is the best policy."

Not if you're a spy. And not if your wife asks, "What are you thinking of, dear?" when what you're thinking of is Raquel Welsh *au naturel*.

13. "Haste makes waste."

In putting out a fire? In slamming on the brakes?

The slow and dopey waste far more than the swift and able.

Rosten's Almanac reminds you: "Haste reduces waists."

14. "Slow and steady wins the race."

Not if you're racing faster runners. I don't care *how* steady you are.

15. "It's the straw that broke the camel's back."

In March, 1977, Professor Abu Ozymandias, chief orthopedist for the California Institute of Technology, received a $2,450,000 grant from the U.S. Department of Health, Education, and Welfare for an experiment designed to find the definitive answer to the question "How many straws are required to break the average camel's back?"

Spinologists enthusiastically applauded the project, and statisticians lauded its experimental design. Ozymandias imported ten healthy camels (*Camelus dromedarius*) from Kuwait and ten gung-ho Arabs from Al-Qafit, and installed them in a specially built hangar on the Mojave Desert. To guarantee heat comparable to that of the native habitat of both beasts and Bedouins, the hangar lacked air-conditioning. Ozymandias stocked the experimental site with hashish for the Arabs, cigarettes for the camels, and 1600 bales of the finest straws money could buy.

On July 4, 1977, at 9:30 A.M., Professor Ozymandias and his Arabic interpreter, Miss Amulla Monsoon, a Ph.D. in petroleum, appeared in the hangar. The ten camels, tethered to floor-irons and munching on vitamin-enriched cuds, stood arrayed in an impressive row. Each *gamal* was flanked by its Arab, in a *jalabiyah* and *kuffiyah*. Next to each fellah was a green-and-yellow basket.

Miss Monsoon loudly wailed: *"La ilaha illa Allah!"*

"La ilaha illa Allah!" cried the Arabs.
"Salaām aleikhum!"
"Aleikhum salaām!" bellowed the Bedouins.
"Let the placing of straws begin!" (I don't know the Arabic for that.)

A roar ascended as the ten Arabs filled their baskets with straw and mounted the ladders. Placing straw after straw on the camels' backs, at the base of the hump, the mullahs chanted, *"Wahid, itsnayn, t'ria,"* et cetera up to *Maah* (one hundred). Then they started the arithmetical count all over.

On August 27, the last straw in the 1600 bales had been used up.

The statistical totals of the great Camelback Experiment, now available from the Government Printing Office, should be studied with care by every honest student of folk sayings:

a. *Not one camel's back was broken!* Because:

b. Four camels developed swaybacks so deep that their bellies rested on the ground, after which added straws did not break their spines, but gave them rashes.

c. One dromedary kept blowing the straws off its back every time its attendant placed one there. When this camel began to accompany his blowing with sneering, the shlemiel killed himself.

d. Three camels remained upright throughout the entire experiment, smiling; they ate the straws off their backs as fast as their frantic flunkeys could place them there.

e. Two dromedaries kept throwing spitballs at Prof. Ozymandias.

f. The median number of straws borne per *gamal* was 98,744.

What happened to the Arabs (besides the one who killed himself) was even more detrimental to the validity of the apothegm:

a. Three Arabs developed paralyzed elbows from all that arm-bending. Pious chiropracters diagnosed the condition as terminal cases of Reacher's Cramp.

b. Two Arabs suffered nervous breakdowns.

c. One hefty Arab, desperate to break his camel's spine, kept jumping up and down on top of the straw on his camel's back. That made the camel so angry it pounded the son of a muezzin into the shape of a mezuzah, in which shameful format the Arab went to meet his Maker.

d. Three Arabs stole out of their folding tents in the hangar one night and fled to the Israeli consulate in Los Angeles. They begged for asylum, so the Israelis placed them in one.

e. That leaves one Arab: Abdullah Bulbul Amir. He is still in the historic hangar on the Mojave, twiddling his thumbs. The Department of Health, Education, and Welfare refused to provide another cent for bales of straw. I think they learned a lot about camels from Camelot.

P.S. Professor Ozymandias died on St. Swithin's eve after *his* back was broken in many places by the puritanical husband of Miss Monsoon, who turned out to have been working nights all through the project as a belly-dancer in Encino.

Ozymandias' chair at Cal Tech is now graced by
Pierre Ausgeshpielt, who is listed in the catalogue as
"Distinguished Professor of."

The ten dromedaries were shipped back somewhere
east of Suez after their date with destiny. And when a
dromedary has no more dates, it's time to switch to figs.

16. "Man's best friend is his dog."

That certainly puts the whole human race in its place:
the doghouse.

Don't let a Jewish mother hear you say that a man's
best friend is his *dog*. Or an Irish mother, for that matter.
And certainly not an Italian mother (*Mamma mia!*) or
a Japanese *haha* (mother), who can't help the way that
sounds in English.

As for me: If man's best friend is a dog, his worst is a
dogma.

17. "Crime doesn't pay."

This bromide, gravely intoned during my schooldays
(along with spine-freezing bodements about the evils of
nicotine and "self-abuse") tempts me to thrup a thrupaci-
ous raspberry.

The only crimes that don't pay are those which were
botched up. We don't know *beans* about the whacking
number of crimes that do pay. How can we? They remain undiscovered.

Crime pays off like crazy to bookkeepers who boodle
accounts; dognappers who steal a pet, then claim the reward; buzzard Lotharios who gull lonely widows; till-
tappers who ring up "No Sale"; glue-fingered glommers

who helpfully reduce the inventory of department stores; talented "icemen" who peddle stolen diamonds; gandy dancers who swindle the credulous; brazen cops un- caught in their weekly collection of pay offs; and all the miscellaneous lamsters, fence-jumpers, credit-card finks and hotel hustlers who lighten the assets of the innocent and the naïve.

The bracing, if lamentable, truth lies in Rosten's Ninth Law: *"Crime doesn't pay unless you're very good at it."*

Neither does playing the fiddle, or using a trampoline.

18. "God helps those who help themselves."

God may help those who help themselves, but the courts are rough as hell on shoplifters.

Imogene Farfel, a first-class kimono-snatcher, being hustled away by a department-store shamus who had caught her pink-handed, protested, "But I am only doing God's work!!" This made no dent on the gumshoe, who was an atheist.

Poor Rosten's Almanac says: "If God helped those who help themselves, those who help themselves wouldn't have to hire expensive lawyers."

19. "Necessity is the mother of invention."

Then how come so many people starve, fry, drown or freeze to death? The deserts, mountains, seas and ceme- teries are chock-full of innocents who, under the most extreme and crucial necessity, couldn't invent a damn thing.

The unvarnished truth (which is getting harder and

harder to come by these days) is recorded in my Law #18: "Necessity may be the mother of invention—but intelligence is its father."

20. "Dead men tell no tales."

Shucks, dead men practically turn blabbermouth the minute a competent coroner cases the corpse. It doesn't matter whether the victim was strangled, poisoned, or sped to Valhalla via forced feedings of halvah: Dead men tell the truth, the whole truth, and nothing but the truth—to anyone who knows how to decipher it.

Professional gunmen, keenly aware of this, used to toss their murderees into cement mixers, thus simultaneously destroying a telltale body and humanizing the highways around Chicago.

One imaginative ganglord won my everlasting admiration by devising an exquisite way of disposing of the enemies his gunsels rubbed out: He secretly bought a fine old funeral parlor which had buried thousands of respectable citizens. From time to time, my hero simply placed a defunct mobster in a coffin *underneath* the body of a blameless client who was about to be returned to the good earth. I regard this double-decker ploy as a high-water mark in the history of problem-solving.

21. "Money can't buy happiness."

Nothing brings happiness to some people; anything brings happiness to others.

By and large, money brings more happiness than does the absence thereof. Prof. Richard Easterlin's meticulous analysis, in *The Public Interest* (1973), should persuade chronic malcontents that the better off people are, the happier they are. They may not be ecstatic, but they are certainly more stable emotionally.

As for myself, I gratefully accept the late Jack (Decca Records) Kapp's quip: "I've been rich and I've been poor. Take my word for it, rich is better."

22. "Absence makes the heart grow fonder."

Not necessarily. Absence can liberate the brain from the heart's maudlin seductions.

And if absence makes the heart grow fonder, what shall we do about "Out of sight, out of mind"?

23. "Early to bed and early to rise makes a man healthy, wealthy and wise."

This is about as hokey a motto as was ever fobbed off as a proverb:

a. *Health.* Some of the sickest people I know get up at dawn and conk out before the seven o'clock news. . . .

b. *Wealth.* Early up and early out won't pay off nearly as well as working far into the night. (Marrying a Mellon or a loaded divorcée is even better.)

c. *Wisdom.* No one ever grew wiser while snoring. It is the insomniacs of this world who use the wee hours for thinking, reading and scheming.

"Early to bed and early to rise" applies only to rural dwellers, in whose case it is description, not advice. They have to turn in early because they're so bushed from being awakened so early. Who can sleep late in the country? Each morning produces an infuriating racket from roosters, dogs, ducks, cows, birds, pigs, kids, slamming screen doors, clattering lawnmowers, backfiring cars.

The truth, which is often painful to hyperthyroids, lies in Rosten's revised vision: "Early to bed and early to rise takes most of the zing out of living."

24. "It never rains but it pours."

Pish-posh. Fiddle-faddle. Alsace–Lorraine.

Sometimes it rains, sometimes it pours and sometimes it does neither.

Transform the ancient maxim: "Never pontificate about the weather; you may be all wet."

25. "Truth is stranger than fiction."

Of course it is: Fiction has to make sense.

My 17th Law reads: "Truth is more fickle than fiction; it doesn't give a damn about being plausible." Even Jules Verne lacked the moxie to dream up a Watergate.

26. "Don't put all your eggs in one basket."

Fischel Phillipotts, a double-jointed podiatrist, retired to run a chicken farm. In no time he had ten eggs. He put two in each of five baskets. Four baskets had no bottoms. He would have been better off if he had put all his eggs in the basket that did.

As *Rosten's Almanac* puts it: "Never put an egg in a basket you haven't tested thoroughly."

27. "The road to hell is paved with good intentions."

It is also full of succulent gratifications.

28. "Opposites attract."

Not as often as they repel. Data compiled by our finest sociological morticians tell a potent tale: The more alike a husband and wife are—in background, education, faith —the more likely it is that their marriage will be stable. Connubial storms are directly correlated with differences in background, religion and tastes.

MORAL: "Opposites may attract, but similarities endure."

29. "A penny saved is a penny earned."

And a penny spent is a penny enjoyed.

30. "A bird in the hand is worth two in the bush."

Only if you're a dum-dum at bargaining. A bird in the hand is worth at least fifty in the bush.

31. "You can lead a horse to water but you can't make him drink."

The hell you can't: Fill his nosebag with salt before you lead him to the trough.

32. ". . . as easy as shooting fish in a barrel."

That's the stupidest way I ever heard of snagging fish who are trapped in barrels. First, you may miss all the fish and hit their monger. Second, at such close range any fish you hit will be blown to such bits there'll be nothing left to eat.

The most sensible way to catch fish in a barrel is to

punch a hole in the staves. It won't take long for the water to run out and the fish to lie gasping. Put away your goddam gun and bend over.

33. "Speech is silver; silence is golden."

Huh? Who would remember Nathan Hale if he had not spoken? Or Will Rogers, who had a silver lasso but a golden wit? Or the hardened convict who opined:

> "Never play cards with a man called 'Doc.'
> Never eat at a place called 'Mom's.'
> And never go to bed with a broad whose troubles
> are bigger than your own."

Poor Rosten's Almanac lays it on the line: "Silence, if practiced long enough, will leave you with no one to talk *to*."

34. "Make hay while the sun shines."

It's easier to steal the hay after the sun goes down.

35. "People who live in glass houses shouldn't throw stones."

That's not all they shouldn't do. They also shouldn't play handball, give their kids toy hammers or make love until nightfall.

Poor Rosten's Almanac is clear as a bell on this chestnut: "People who live in glass houses shouldn't get stoned."

36. "Go to the ant, thou sluggard, and observe his ways and be wise."

Oh, my aching back. Ever since the Book of Proverbs (6:6) advised all of us sluggards to go to the ant and observe his ways "and be wise," mankind has not observed the ways of ants carefully, and is scarcely wise.

Any authority on ants, if not on Holy Scripture, will tell you that ants often lie around inert and dopey for hours at a time. They are not the busy, tireless little beasties of legend; in fact, many ants are downright lazy.

Rosten's 34th Law reads: "Go to the sluggard, thou ant, and don't follow his example."

37. "The facts speak for themselves."

I'll give $10,000 to anyone who ever heard a fact speak. I'll give $20,000 to anyone who ever heard a fact sigh.

The fact is that facts are completely dumb. They cannot argue. They have no brains, no soul, no purpose beyond mere existence. They are utterly meaningless until appraised, arranged, analyzed and interpreted—by us.

Facts are not truths. They are not conclusions. They are not even conclusive. Judge this for yourself in the juicy paragraphs which follow, and you will never cry *Res ipsa loquitur!*

38. "Facts don't lie."

But facts can flagrantly deceive. They are often nowhere as fact-y as they seem. Our gullibility converts puny facts into potent fallacies. In fact, it is a fact that one of the most important facts about facts is how absurdly they can be interpreted. Don't believe Ovid: *Credite nebur* ("Believe the facts").

Example: At a recent conference of over 2000 delegates, *one-fourth* of all the Negroes were married to white women! Now remove the exclamation point and calm your Southern dander: There were four Negroes at the conference; one male had married a white woman.

Example: 87.6 percent of the occupants of state prisons are avid readers of comic books. Does this mean that reading comic books leads lunkheads into a life of crime? Or does it mean that criminals have the kind of mentality that gravitates to comic books? 93.4 percent of the prisoners brush their teeth each morning, too, but I doubt that anyone outside the Mao Tse-tung Brigade would be silly enough to maintain that there is a correlation between oral hygiene and moral turpitude.

"A crucial fact about facts is how they were corralled," says *Rosten's Reader.* Take the statistics given above (four Negroes at the conference; 87.6 percent of prisoners read comics; 93.4 percent brush their teeth): I made them up.

39. "You can't argue with the facts."

Hooey. Most of the dazzling discoveries in science were made by oddballs who did little *except* argue with the "facts"—that is, with the prevailing explanation of poorly observed or imperfectly understood phenomena.

Example: We all see the sun rise in the east each morning; we see it move across the heavens; we see it slide below the horizon. The sun's motion around the earth appears to be as self-evident and indisputable as a visible event can be—but Copernicus showed us how cockeyed this interpretation is. (If you lived on the sun, it would be as plain as Cyrano's nose that the earth moved around you.)

Example: In the early twenties, the per capita death rate in the borough of Manhattan was far higher than the death rate in the borough of Queens, just across the East River. The mortality figures supported this beyond a shadow of a doubt.

But Napoleon Pilpul, a senior at Yeshiva U., figured that doubts can't cast shadows and decided to argue with the facts, which annoyed him.

What he discovered is scrumptious: There were no decent hospitals in Queens; so when its wiser inhabitants came down with a serious sickness they sped across the Fifty-ninth Street Bridge to Manhattan, where they died.

Rosten's Almanac advises: "Don't believe a 'fact' until you've factified it."

40. "Politics makes strange bedfellows."

Not any stranger than marriages, concupiscence, college-class reunions or national conventions. Politics also makes strange Rockefellers.

Rosten's Law 19 ruefully runs: "Our world is so full of nuts, freaks, fruitcakes and fanatics that any activity involving more than eight persons is sure to contain an astonishing percentage of screwballs." Law 20 plunges on to observe: "When screwballs fornicate, it demonstrates the power of a pun."

41. "Neither a borrower nor a lender be."

That leaves only barter, which is a helluva way to run an economy. Unless, of course, you want zero growth.

42. "Strike while the iron is hot."

Why wait that long? By the time you've heated the iron your target can be heading for the border.

You can brain someone you don't like with a cold iron as effectively as with a hot iron. I say: "If you want to strike, don't waste time standing over a stove."

43. "It's a wise father who knows his own child."

And it takes a virtuous mother to know her child's father.

44. "He who hesitates is lost."

And he who does not hesitate falls off a ladder.

What ever happened to "Look before you leap"?

Rosten's Almanac makes no bones about concluding: "He who hesitates will lose fewer fingers than he who uses a chain saw in a hurry."

45. "To understand all is to forgive all." (Tout comprendre c'est tout pardonner.)

Not in my case. The more I understand some people, the less I like, much less forgive, them. Even a psychoanalyst can't like or let up on *all* his patients.

Rosten's Law 22 maintains: "If you really want to understand anyone, don't start with a pious bias in his favor."

46. "The early bird gets the worm."

Big deal. Late sleepers stay up planning things more important than catching *worms*, for God's sake. Besides, my *Almanac* observes: "Only a birdbrain would want to eat a slimy invertebrate."

Now look at it from the worm's point of view. The early bird gets the early worm; hence it is clearly in a worm's best interest to stay underground snoozing while all those early birds peck away at all the worms who were stupid enough to go to work too soon.

I give you the rumination of John Geoffrey Saxe or Sake (1816–1887):

> I like the lad, who when his father thought
> To clip his morning nap by hackneyed phrase
> Of vagrant worm by early songster caught,
> Cried, "Served him right! It's not at all surpising:
> The worm was punished, sir, for early rising."

47. "A word to the wise is sufficient."

That depends on the word—and the wise. General McAuliffe's retort to the German besiegers of Bastogne who demanded that his outnumbered, surrounded force surrender ("Nuts!") was not sufficient; the Krauts kept bombing his position, did not prevail and paid for their bull-headedness. Their general was a *hoch gelehrte* graduate of Heidelberg.

48. "Practice makes perfect."

Guff. If you haven't fantastic talent, practice will make you perfectly miserable.

Take these unhappy examples: From their childhood on, Pablo Casals, Billie Jean King and Willie Sutton practiced like crazy. None achieved perfection: Casals sometimes fell into peculiar tempi, Ms. King hits umpteen balls into the net, and Willie Sutton, who robbed banks as neatly as anyone on record, spent most of his adult life in the clink.

Rosten's reprise puts it bluntly: "All the practice in the world won't turn a plumber into Paganini."

49. "A stitch in time saves nine."

I let a tailor sew all my stitches, because I long ago learned that the minute I start fooling around with needle and thread I act penny-wise, pound-foolish, dollar-dumb and doctor-poor. You wouldn't believe the medical bills I've run up for blood poisoning.

The *Almanac* advises: "To 'a stitch in time' say '*Nein.*'"

50. "You can't make a silk purse out of a sow's ear."

Anyone stupid enough to think you can shouldn't try his hand at epigrams.

51. "An apple a day keeps the doctor away."

I once knew an accomplished hypochondriac, yclept Nate Kochleffl. At the age of twenty-eight, Kochleffl decided to eat nothing but apples. He kicked the bucket before he hit twenty-nine: pernicious anemia, aggravated by pectin poisoning.

Rosten's Rule 34: "If an apple a day keeps the doctor away, why are there so many doctors in Oregon?"

52. "No man is a hero to his valet."

So? There is no more reason to expect a valet to understand a hero than there is to expect a barnacle to explain a hull. If valets had talent, they would have valets of their own.

Like most servants, valets adore you if you pay them too much, flatter them too often and give them expensive presents. These are ignoble grounds for admiration.

Rosten's 44th Law proclaims: "A valet's testimony tells you more about valets than heroes."

53. "Politics is a dirty business."

Is that because businessmen have to deal with dirty politicians?

54. "A rolling stone gathers no moss."

But what does an inert stone gain from all the moss it accumulates? No one has ever explained this.

55. "Never look a gift horse in the mouth."

Heavens to Betsy! *Always* look a gift horse in the mouth. He may need enough orthodontistry to bankrupt you.

Remember what happened to the Trojans.

56. "Man is born free, yet everywhere is in chains."

This ringing line from Rousseau has long been revered by young rebels, old Socialists and middle-aged dentists. The apothegm, which brought a lump to my throat when first I read it (I was seventeen), is noble, moving and preposterous.

Man is not born free. Man is born totally helpless, totally incompetent, totally dependent and totally ignorant. Man is born a slave—at the complete mercy of adults who must feed, rear, protect and instruct him for years and years before he can make it on his own.

Oh, I know that Rousseau's "free" referred to legal rights and status, but the mindless parroting of nonsense as if it were truth gives me a bellyache.

57. "Always tell the truth."

What a foolish, awful, heartless injunction. Life would be horrible if we all went around telling each other the truth.

Can you really tell your excessively homely daughter that she is no sight for sore eyes? Should you tell a sensitive friend that he has such bad breath that he ought to bottle it and send it to the Division of Chemical Warfare? Would you tell a child that he/she may not live through the night? Dare you tell your wife, just before you both leave for an important dinner, that the new dress with which she surprises you would look better on Halloween? Are you foolhardy enough to tell your boss that his latest idea would go over great in a psycho ward? Should you tell your husband that you have been toying with the idea of putting poison in his mother's soup?

The truth is so precious, said Winston Churchill (vis-à-vis wartime propaganda), that it must be protected by "a bodyguard of lies." The truth is sometimes so bitter, so painful, so unjust, say I, that it must not be revealed to those who would only be shattered to hear it.

58. "Spare the rod and spoil the child."

Well, walloping the young undoubtedly makes some parents, tabloid editorialists and Kallikaks *feel* better, but the consequences of severe corporal punishment are something else again. Psychologists and criminologists have bagged enough evidence by now to make a very strong case for the likelihood that the more severely you wallop the young, the more fractious and delinquent they turn out. (You can find more on this depressing subject in a monograph by Sears, Whiting and Nowlis, entitled *Some Child-Rearing Antecedents of Aggression and Dependency*.)

Please note that I am talking about beating, thrashing, using a "rod"—and not about mild, run-of-the-mill or Scarsdale-type spanking, for which I can make out a pretty good case.

Rosten's Law runs: "Spanking is better than not spanking *if you are mad enough to want to*."

We should burn incense before George Bernard Shaw's edict, the soundest words I know on this theme: "Never strike a child in cold blood."

59. "Behind every great man is a woman."

I yield to no man in my affection for females, young or old, but a careful reading of biographies compels me to suspect that behind every great man is a nag.

60. "There's a destiny that shapes our ends."

Mebbe. But a more likely destiny is the one that ends our shapes.

61. "Virtue is its own reward."

Uh huh.

2.
IT
JUST
AIN'T SO!

**"George Washington's Farewell
Address was Mount Vernon."**

—H*Y*M*A*N K*A*P*L*A*N

Frank ("Kipn") Hubbard, one of the wittiest columnists the hinterland ever enriched us with, once cracked: " 'Tain't what a man don't know that hurts him; it's what he knows that just ain't so."

I find it hard to think of a sounder precept—except for the moral contained in the story of the woman at a cocktail party who cooed to her husband, "Don't you think you ought to stop drinking, dear? Your face is beginning to look fuzzy."

I now give you a bubbly batch of ideas, phrases, "facts" and blithe asseverations which are rarely, if ever, challenged.

"The taste of onions . . ."

I was stricken pink when I ran across the electrifying revelation that we never "taste" onions; we smell them. We *think* we taste an onion because our taste buds and smell sensors operate in such a crowded area, and show such sympathy for each other's problems, that one often masquerades as the other, just as the other, in turn, fills in for the one.

Our central nervous system is a nervous sentinel, and an onion is only one of its deceivers.

"Mush! Mush!"

No Eskimo outside of Hollywood ever tried to start up a dogteam by hollering "Mush! Mush!" If he did, the huskies would be baffled and squat on their duffs.

In Alaska, any prospector who yelled "Mush! Mush!" would be taken for a creep with a craving for oatmeal.

Well, how *do* they get a dogteam going up near the Arctic circle? I think they crack a whip or shout "Ya-ah!," "Wahoo!" or "Git movin'!"

"It is shaped like an egg."

Which egg? Believe it or not, not all eggs are ovoid: "egg-shaped." For example: Owls' eggs are distinctly unlike chicken eggs; swallows lay eggs with slightly pointed ends; whippoorwills produce oval eggs; the eggs of the snipe are pear-shaped and the wak-wak's eggs are cubes!

I have not yet found a species that lays trapezoid eggs, but that's no reason to go on assuming that all eggs are shaped like those hens cackle over.

P.S. A hen's egg is not exactly "ovoid": Mr. Marshall Smith, measuring carefully, concluded that the only way to describe a hen's egg is to call it spheroid with one end prolate (like a watermelon) and the other "very close to spherical."

I'm sorry I brought the whole thing up.

"Lightning never strikes the same place twice."

Oh, dear. The chastening fact is that lightning *prefers* "the same place," if that place serves as a good conductor.

The mast of the Empire State Building, for instance, was hit by lightning sixty-eight times in ten years, according to Professor Bergen Evans. I'll bet that your Aunt Becky, who lives four blocks away, hasn't been hit once in seventy-eight years. Reason? She's shorter, and nonmetallic.

When lightning hits a church steeple, please don't be overly impressed by the good folk who conclude that God is trying to tell us something. He can come right out and say it, if He wants to—and I often wonder why He doesn't.

"The Immaculate Conception tells us that Jesus was born of a virgin . . ."

Wrong. The Immaculate Conception refers to the birth of *Mary*. It holds that Mary, from the moment of her conception in the body of *her* mother, Ann, was free of original sin. It is the Virgin Birth that refers to the birth of Jesus.

The dogma of the Immaculate Conception was not officially enunciated until December 8, 1854 (!) by Pope Pius IX.

(Incidentally, do you know Mary's true name—*i.e.*, in Hebrew? It was Miriam. Do you know the name of Mary's father? Joachim.)

"The best way to get rid of a corpse is to bury it in quick-lime, which will make it disappear."

I know you will hate me, crime-lovers, but LeMoyne Snider, author of the imposing *Homicide Investigation*, saddened me, too, with the unwelcome revelation that corpses do not dissolve in quicklime—except in mystery novels and foolish folklore. As if that isn't enough, killjoy Snider goes on to demonstrate that quicklime combines with fatty tissue in such a way that it makes a corpse "resistant to the usual putrefactive changes." In other words, quicklime helps preserve a body.

I sometimes wonder if the beady-eyed experts of this world will leave us any gaudy uncertainties in which to repose an unexamined faith.

"When the Israelites crossed the Red Sea . . ."

They never did. The fleeing Israelites were nowhere near the Red Sea during their miraculous deliverance. They left Egypt and entered Sinai about a hundred miles north of the Red Sea, very near the very shore of the Mediterranean.

"Red Sea" is a blatant boner in translation. I wish I could say it was simply a matter of reading "red" for "reed." It wasn't: The ancient Hebrews knew no English. (How could they? The language did not then exist.)

"I jumped when I hit my funny bone . . ."

You did not. What you hit was your ulnar nerve, which runs close to the skin on that supersensitive spot on your elbow. Whenever you hit the ulnar nerve, you get an electrifying shock.

Why is so unpleasant a sensation attributed to a "funny" bone? Because of the bone's relation to the humerus, which extends from the elbow to the shoulder. Galen listed "the four humors," meaning the fluids in the body that govern temperament, as: choleric, melancholy, phlegmatic, and sanguine.

In Latin and Old French, *humere* and *humeur* respectively mean moisture (hence, our "humid"), but don't let that dampen your spirit.

"... blind as a bat."

But most bats are not blind. They see rather well. They just don't need to use their eyes as we do because they use sonar to locate themselves: They send out high-pitched squeaks whose frequencies are 50,000 cycles per second (human ears hear only up to around 20,000) and it is the echoes of these signals, bouncing back from solid surfaces or objects, that tell a bat exactly where what is. That's why bats don't bang against the walls or protuberances of pitch-black caves.

The invaluable squeaking also enables bats to zero in on their food. They eat insects on the fly. (They also eat flies.) It is quite remarkable that no matter how tiny a food is flying around, even a mosquito, the echo-bounces locate it with precision. The technique is called echolocation, naturally. *Ecco.*

"Mice love cheese."

Any twelve-year-old will tell you that mice prefer cheese to any other food. As in so many other fields, don't pay attention to what twelve-year-olds tell you. Mice are not gaga about cheese—unless it's the only food available.

We must all be brave enough to face up to the results

of a recent historic experiment. When vast colonies of mice were offered a variety of yummy foods, including the most pungent Limburger and the time-hallowed "rat cheese"—guess what their favorite was?

Gumdrops. Don't argue with me; see *The Cheese Book* by Marquis and Haskel. Gumdrops!

"Hyenas and jackals are terrible scavengers."

Not according to Hugo Van Lawick and Jane Van Lawick-Goodall's delightful *Innocent Killers* (Ballantine Books). Hyenas, jackals and wild dogs usually hunt, kill and eat their own prey; scavenging is a rather small part of their total diet. The authors of *Innocent Killers* ought to know. They live near and with the creatures they so patiently study and photograph.

"Dry cleaning . . ."

. . . isn't dry. It is chemical—and wet. Clothes that are "dry-cleaned" are immersed in a fluid: carbon tetrachloride, naphtha, trichloroethylene, etcetera.

"Oranges came to Europe from Florida and California, after the New World was discovered."

It's the other way around. Christopher Columbus brought oranges *to* the New World. He spread orange seeds all through the Antilles. In fact, every Spanish sailor bound for the New World was ordered by law to carry one hundred orange seeds with him! (I got all this from John McPhee's *Oranges*, which I'm glad he wrote.)

"The twinkling stars . . ."

Stars don't twinkle. They don't wink or blink, either. The twinkling is a beautiful effect created by the atmosphere between the stars and our eyes.

"Lifting weights makes you 'musclebound.' "

Not according to Dr. Fred Allman, recent president of the American College of Sports Medicine and orthopedic consultant to the Athletic Department of the University of Georgia. Any increase in strength improves athletic performance. In fact, Dr. Allman recommends that weight-lifting begin at an early age. I'm glad my father never knew this.

"She's skinny because she eats like a bird . . ."

If she eats like a bird, she must weigh a ton. Birds are *enormous* eaters.

Take Robin Redbreast. (Technically speaking, he is not a robin but a thrush; and whoever calls a robin a thrush *is* speaking technically.) Well, young robins practically never stop eating.

Adult robins are just as great fools about food. They *gorge*—even on rotting, fermenting fruits. Yet, they certainly do get plastered. A lush thrush literally staggers around like a drunk on Forty-second Street. I prefer the bird to the bum.

"Alexander Graham Bell invented the telephone . . ."

He did not. Nor did he ever say he had. What Bell did was both improve the instrument so greatly that it became practical, and extol its possibilities with such enthusiasm that it became popular.

Who did invent the phone? Johann Reis, a German physicist, who constructed a telephone in 1860—"but did not follow up the idea." (E. F. Carter, *Dictionary of Inventions*.)

What tantalizes me is that Alexander Graham Bell received his patent for the telephone in 1876—and Elisha Gray patented his phone just two hours later!

None of all this will be found in the feckless movie starring Don Ameche.

"Vampire bats suck human blood."

Wrong. The worst a bat will do is nick an arm or leg. The nick is so small it closes quickly. The only danger from bat nicks is infection—which is more than you can say about batnicks who go around scaring little girls to death with horror stories.

"The tiniest sovereign state in the world is Liechtenstein. Or San Marino."

The tiniest sovereign state on the globe is neither. It is a house—a house in Rome: number 68 on the Via Condotti. The mansion embraces the independent territory of the Sovereign Military Order of Malta, which issues its own passports, has its own diplomatic corps, and even uses its own license plates, embossed SMOM.

The autonomous Order was founded 800 years ago, as the Knights Hospitalliers of Jerusalem, to protect and succor pilgrims to the Holy Land during the Crusades. The Knights were a remarkable army of pious soldiers who seized the strategic island of Rhodes, which they made a fortress and held for 200 years before the Muslims conquered it.

The Knights of Malta remain unfazed by history.

"The Bible tells us 'Spare the rod and spoil the child.'..."

No. The Bible does not. Nor is this, as one might assume, an old proverb.

Proverbs 13:24 runs: "He that spareth his rod hateth his son"—which is not at all the same as spoiling him.

Then who first wrote "Spare the rod and spoil the child"? According to Tom Burnam it was Samuel Butler (the first, not second, Samuel Butler). You will find the "biblical" quotation in *Hudibras*, the mock-heroic poem which savaged the Puritans. Butler published it in three parts: 1663, 1664, 1678.

Next.

"He punted the pigskin..."

Not on any football field I know of. Footballs are made of cowhide, not pigskin. (I suppose footballs *were* made of pigskin when Stover was at Yale.)

"Indian snake-charmers put snakes into a trance by the music..."

Snakes don't hear music. They don't hear old wives' tales, either. They don't hear flattery, insults, toasts or curses. They don't hear anything. They have no ears.

What the snakes in India respond to is the weaving movement of the snake-charmer's pipe.

It Just Ain't So!

"Nero fiddled while Rome burned."

So said Suetonius, but he was a patsy for gossip.

Tacitus, a more reliable historian, says that Nero was fifty miles from Rome when the great fire broke out and, moreover, rushed back to the capital to do what he could to control the spreading of the flames.

"The black widow spider's sting can be fatal . . ."

Only the sting of the females. Male black widow spiders are unable to harm people. I draw no chauvinist-pig conclusions from this.

"Noah Webster's dictionary . . ."

Noah Webster named his great work *The American Dictionary*.

There are dozens of "Webster's" Dictionaries, because the name cannot be copyrighted, but I know of no Noah Webster's.

"Copernicus discovered that the earth moves around the sun . . ."

Copernicus was anticipated by a good many theorists, of whom the first probably was Aristarchus of Samos (310–250 B.C.). Copernicus' genius lay not in what he discovered but in what he theorized.

"The Chinese invented fireworks."

Guess what? Jack M. Duffield, the leading producer of spectacular fireworks in the United States, a man who has read widely and deeply in the history of his trade, insists that it was the Greeks, not the Chinese, who invented fireworks:

> The Chinese invented gunpowder, it's true, and by extension, possibly fire*crackers*. But there is very little gunpowder in fireworks. There are, however, chemical compounds and, in some cases, metals. The ancient Greeks ground up metal into powder and would throw it into a fire.... They had colored fires which are really the basis of fireworks. Later, these colored fires were used as part of their ceremonials.

The Greeks, the Greeks. Will their wonders never cease?

"The new name for Persia, Iran . . ."

Iran is the old name. "Persia" was a Greek name for one of ancient Iran's provinces, "Pars." But the inhabitants of Persia have always called their country Iran. I ran into this nugget whilst browsing through Brewer's dandy *Dictionary of Phrase and Fable*.

"In the winter, when the sun is farthest from the earth . . ."

Uh-uh. In winter the sun is closest to the earth. The sun is farthest from our globe in the good old summertime.

The distance between sun and earth does not decide our weather. What causes hot summers or cold winters is —oh, look it up yourself.

"Galileo invented the telescope..."

Galileo *made* a telescope, in 1609—but that was a full year after a Dutch optician, Hans Lippershey, had invented the marvelous device for viewing far-off objects.

I will concede that it was Galileo who developed the doo-dad into an instrument for astronomical observations: in 1610 he improved one to give magnifications of thirty-three diameters. Lippershey never came within praising distance of that.

"I felt like a worm..."

Then you felt like a creature who, judged by its variety of form and capacity to survive incredible hazards, is one of the proudest and most remarkable beings on our globe.

Why, the female Threadworm, which is under half an inch long, can lay 12,000 eggs at a crack. Some worms go without food for a year—subsisting on their own cells. And some worms break themselves into pieces if in danger (or if they mistakenly "think" they are in danger)—and each of the pieces regenerates itself into a new, perfect, functioning creature. Show me a man or woman who can do that.

You might say—in fact, I do say—that the only thing lowly about worms is their height.

"Only a female can give birth..."

To what?

Among Chilean frogs and unchilly seahorses, the females lay their eggs *in* the male, blithely saddling him with the monotony, burden and awkwardness of pregnancy.

Nor do females necessarily raise and care for their young. In almost all the species of fish, the rearing and protecting duties are assumed by daddy.

"The most famous line in the classic movie 'Casablanca' was Humphrey Bogart's 'Play it again, Sam.' "

That line certainly has become the most famous. There one catch: Bogie never said it.

What he said, after a tense exchange with Dooley Wilson, the piano player, was *"Play* it, Sam!"

"Carrier pigeons have a faultless homing instinct."

Everyone "knows" that homing or carrier pigeons possess an instinctive ability to find their way home across hundreds of alien miles and unfamiliar terrain. And what everyone knows, in this case, is fictitious.

Homing pigeons have to be trained—carefully, slowly, step by step—to find their way back home. They must have a sort of roadmap imprinted on their little brains. If you carry them beyond landmarks already known to them, the poor things may not get back at all. They are pigeons for ignorance.

Homing pigeons, please remember, are not migratory birds, which do have remarkable powers of endurance and orientation.

It is a matter of historical record (terribly upsetting to pigeon fanciers) that six healthy carrier pigeons of impeccable character, veterans in the Signal Corps, were released from the beach at Normandy on D-Day. Not one of them made it back to base in England—which wasn't very far for a member of Carrier Pigeon Local No. 1 to fly, *if* he knew where the hell he was going. The Sad Six clearly did not.

Indignant trainers of pigeons will undoubtedly protest this libel of our feathered friends. Experts will claim to have trained pigeons to find their way home from as far as fifty miles. I have no doubt the pigeons might have done so across the English Channel—if the Germans on the continental side had only allowed the pigeons and their trainers to hold classes *in situ* for several months before D-Day.

"We heard an SOS—'Save Our Ship!'—on our radio."

What you heard was three dots, three dashes, three dots. Those signals in Morse code stand for SOS. But the letters were chosen only because their Morse form is so easy to remember and to punch out, over and over, without changing.

The letters were not meant to stand for a damn thing —not "Save Our Ship!" nor "Save Our Souls!" not even "Send Out Sandwiches."

The inevitable romantic need of our species seized upon "SOS" and made it mean what everyone and his cousin seem to think it means. Maybe it should. It's much more dramatic than "Three dots, three dashes, three dots, three dashes . . ."

"Children have no sense about food. If left to themselves, they would choose a diet that's bad for their health."

In a delightful experiment, three six-to-twelve-month-old babies, newly weaned, were fed from trays that contained twelve to twenty different foodstuffs. They could choose whichever food they wanted. The experiment continued for six months to a year.

What happened? The three babies chose nutritious and "sensible" foods. They gained more weight than is the norm for their age level. One tot, who had rickets, automatically chose substantial quantities of cod-liver oil. The rickets subsided.

Maybe Mother Nature has more sense than ignorant alarmists give her credit for.

"... as weak as a flea."

You should be so strong. A high-jumping flea will leap fifty to a hundred times its body length and height. Translate that into human terms and it means we could jump 275 feet high—to land 450 feet away.

"Slums and poverty breed crime."

In the early decades of this century, when the Lower East Side of New York was the most heavily populated section of the United States, and when its poverty and overcrowding aroused the horrified protests of many a reformer, its crime rate was the lowest in the city. According to one sociologist, "it was safe to walk the streets at night."

Lord Justice John Widgery of England's Court of Appeals told the American Bar Association that the British had wiped out most of their poverty in the welfare state and had eliminated most of their slums when they were repairing the vast bombing damage of World War II—yet crime has been rising just as fast in Great Britain as anywhere else. "Anyone who believes that relief of poverty will bring a decrease in crime is in for grave disappointment."

"American cowboys loved to sing 'Yippee, coyote, get along you little doggies.' "

Hold it. Cowboys didn't sing about dogs or doggies. They sang about pathetic calves, prematurely weaned because of their mothers' death, who swelled up because they could not digest their food properly. The motherless calves were called "dough-guts"—which shrank to "dogies."

The famous cowboy ballad goes:

> As I was out walking
> One morning, for pleasure,
> I saw a young cowboy
> Come ridin' along,
> His hat was pushed back
> An' his spurs were ajingle,
> And as he was ridin'
> He sang out this song:
>
> "Yippee, coyote,
> Git along, you little dogies,
> It's your misfortune
> An' none of my own,
>
> "Yippee, coyote,
> Git along, you little dogies,
> I'm off to Wyoming
> To see my old home."

That, at least, is the way I heard cowboys sing it in various dude ranches I frequented when I was young and rode tall in the saddle and dreamed of Doc Holliday and Billy the Kid and Dawn Ginsberg, S. J. Perelman's trail-blazing buckaroo.

I can't conceive of a cowpuncher ballad that would be as appealing as the one I heard if it ran

> "Yippee, coyote,
> Git along you little dough-guts...."

"Rattlesnakes, exceptionally swift in slithering and striking, grow a new rattle a year..."

R-r-r-really? Rattlesnakes crawl rather slowly, they strike rather slowly, and the number of rattles on their tail is no reliable sign of their age.

I bring you even worse tidings: The far-famed bite of the rattlesnake is rarely fatal. Mind you, it is not pleasant or cause for hand-clapping or group merriment; the bite leaves a wound you must take seriously. The venom *is* poisonous. But only a tiny percentage of rattler-bites turn out to be lethal. (Proof? See Laurence Klauber's two-volume study of the serpent: *Rattlesnakes: Their Habits, Life Histories and Influence on Mankind*, published by the University of California Press in 1952.)

"Columbus gambled that the earth is round, not flat, so he sailed westward—"

Hold it. In the late fifteenth century any seaman worth his salt (so to speak) knew that the earth is not flat. We know that Columbus owned and many times read Cardinal d'Ailley's *Imago Mundi*, which summarized the geographical knowledge of his time—including many demonstrations that the world is a globe.

What Columbus feared was not that his ships would fall off the edge of a flat earth but that (1) he might encounter "monsters of the deep" who would smash his ships and eat his crews or (2) he would run out of water before he could sail all the way back to the Canary Islands. Who can blame him?

"When we sleep, our brains rest."

N-no. Research in various "sleep laboratories" shows that everyone dreams during sleep (whether you remember the dream or not after awakening), and that while dreaming, heartbeat and respiration usually increase.

Your brain uses up more energy in a nightmare than it does in an easy chair, watching TV or reading most best-selling novels.

"Jerusalem is the Holy City . . ."

To Jews and Christians. If you are Muslim, Mecca is a holy city, too, and so is Medina: Muhammad was born in the first and buried in the second.

To Western Arabs, Fez is the Holy City. To Hindus, Benares is. In case you were an Inca, Cuzco would have been your Holy City. If you are a Mithraist . . . but I'd better stop while I'm ahead.

"To prevent colds, stay warm and dry in the winter."

Staying warm and dry is more pleasant than being cold and wet, but it plays no part in your not catching a cold. That's not my opinion, but the conclusion of eminent dotcors at Baylor University's College of Medicine who published (in the *New England Journal of Medicine*) the results of extensive experiments. They found:

1. You can keep cold and damp—*or* warm and dry— and you'll catch a cold if a common cold virus is around.
2. The environment does not affect either the catching, the frequency, the severity or the duration of colds.
3. Cold weather *does* have this important indirect effect: It drives people indoors or keeps them there more than warm weather does. And indoors, people are most likely to breathe the cold viruses exhaled or sneezed out by others!

"The male is stronger than the female . . ."

That depends on what you mean by "stronger."

1. In the first year of life, boy babies die a third more often than girl babies do.
2. A very high percentage of aborted embryos are male.
3. By the time we reach old age, there are almost twice as many widows as widowers. Look around.

"The Bible describes Lucifer as the Prince of Darkness."

The Bible never mentions Lucifer—not as the prince of darkness, nor as a pseudonym for the Devil, nor as an evil angel. Only one Lucifer appears in the Old and New Testaments, and he was a King of Babylon. Isaiah 14:12 describes his downfall, "fallen from the heaven, O Day Star, son of Dawn [Hebrew scholars prefer 'Shining

One' to 'Day Star']." The reference is believed to be to Venus, the morning star. But no authority quite understands why the Day Star or the Son of Dawn should be a synonym for the Babylonian monarch.

"Robert Fulton's historic steamboat, the 'Clermont' . . ."

Oops. The historic steamboat was not christened "Clermont." Mr. Fulton, a gifted inventor, engineer and painter (I'll bet you didn't know that), named his new-fangled craft *The North River Steam Boat*.

How did "Clermont" get attached to the vessel? Because Clermont (N.Y.) was its port of registry; an exuberant journalist goofed, or just gussied up the facts. The misnomer has been perpetuated ever since with the gusto of inexactitude.

"The potato was brought to America from Ireland."

I know you'll either snort or snarl, especially if you're Irish, when I declare that the potato is not indigenous to Ireland. There were no spuds at all in the green isle until the sixteenth century.

Potatoes were brought *to* Ireland from North Carolina. And you'd never guess who transported the starchy staple from the New World to the Old: Walter Raleigh.

The very word "potato" is derived from a Haitian word for a variety of sweet potato which the Spanish marauders in the Caribbean called *batata*.

"The Three Wise Men . . ."

They were not philosophers or notably *wise*; they were astrologers, or soothsayers. They may have been paragons of wisdom, of course, but the translators who rendered the Greek *mago* or the Latin *magi* as "wise men" were plumb wrong. As wrong as the scholar who interpreted Matthew 6:27 as "[adding] one cubit unto his stature." A cubit was eighteen inches.

"I never dream."
"I rarely dream."

People who think they never dream are dreaming. So are strong-jawed citizens who think they rarely dream. Both groups ought to keep up with the exciting research in this drowsy field.

Students of sleep, a growing, wide-awake lot, insist that everyone dreams. And we dream every night. And we usually dream not once a night, but four to five times.

For a slew of sleep-arresting tidbits, see the meticulous reports of Drs. N. Kleitman, W. Dement and others. I, for one, take great comfort from the knowledge that a man named Dement is prowling around in my dreams.

"Cleopatra, the great Egyptian beauty . . ."

She was not Egyptian. She was not a great beauty. Cleopatra was a Macedonian *Chotchka* with not an eye-dropper of Egyptian blood in her many veins. The Romans rated her beauty as fair-to-middlin'.

You can judge Cleopatra's pulchritude for yourself: her statue (probably authentic) is in the Vatican gallery, brought there from the ancient Temple of Venus Genetrix. I have studied the lady many times. I saw no beauty to make me swoon. That Caesar and Antony did should be chalked up to the queen's intelligence, wit,

seductive charms—and the juicy amount of riches, political leverage and military power at her command.

"The perfect hand."

Suppose you're playing poker and pick up a royal flush.
Or suppose you're playing bridge and pick up thirteen
spades. I have no doubt that your heart would leap, your
throat grow dry, your mind resolve never to forget this
once-in-a-lifetime moment. After all, a hand of thirteen
spades can sanctify a mortal only once in 635 *billion*
deals of the cards. Isn't that astonishing?

Not in the slightest. Warren Weaver, a crackerjack
mathematician, loves to chasten us with the obvious
(once you've thought about it) reminder that *each and
every arrangement of cards in the statistical array of 635
billion chances is equally likely to end in your hands.*

Let me put it another way: *Any* set of cards you pick
up in bridge will come up exactly as often as any other:
once every 635 billion times. "The improbable is rare,
but should not be surprising."

The most surprising part of all this, to me at least, is
that Dr. Weaver made his point in an essay printed in the
journal *Pediatrics* (Vol. 38), which I consider a pretty
unlikely spock for an article on statistics.

". . . as dumb as an ox . . ."

Not according to Professor John J. Teal, Jr., of the
University of Alaska.

The musk ox, which happens to be the first hoofed
critter to be domesticated in 5,000 years, is playful, affectionate, and "fiendishly clever," according to Dr. Teal,

and the ungainly musk ox quickly learns how to pick the lock on the gates of its corral. It's the first time I ever heard of oxen doing anything as original as that. The musk is not a dumb ox. In fact, the musk ox is neither musky nor an ox. The bovine ruminant is related to the goat, on the evolutionary tree, belonging somewhere between a sheep and an ox. I'd call it a shox.

"There are more automobile accidents on dark and foggy nights than in bright, sunny weather."

Could any statement be more plausible? Well, like many another seemingly plausible statement, it is false: There are far more accidents on sunny days.

Does this strike you as illogical, or impossible to accept? Then think for a moment: (1) There are far more sunny days than foggy days in the United States; (2) a great many more people drive their cars on sunny days than do on dark and foggy nights. More cars, more chances of collision. More chances, more accidents.

You must be as suspicious as Eurylochus where figures are concerned: "More automobile accidents" does not mean a higher *proportion* of accidents—that is, number of accidents per number of cars on the road. There are a great many more automobile accidents in Los Angeles than in Chagrin Falls, Ohio. Something would be mighty peculiar if that weren't so.

"Mules are by nature stubborn and cantankerous."

Mules are stubborn and ill-tempered if, like their masters, they have been brought up badly. Mules are quite sensitive creatures; when their early years have been characterized by kind treatment "their behavior is incomparable."

Despite all the bad-mouthing to which it has been exposed, the much-maligned mule is an admirable critter: quite intelligent, very brave, as sound of constitution as it is sure of foot and able to resist hardships (climate, hunger, thirst) much better than the beautiful but dumb horse. But mules do not like to have their ears stroked, as horses do. And unlike the horse, mules just will not accept unfair treatment. They are so independent that in time we may accept the simile: "As independent as a mule."

"Crimes, suicides and divorces increase sharply in troubled times, especially during a war."

Oddly enough, the evidence points exactly in the other direction. Crimes, suicides, divorces—all increase during untroubled and relatively affluent times.

"Robberies and burglaries go up in times of prosperity."

Wrong again. Those vices are versa.

"Kids need discipline or they become delinquents."

Mebbe so, but parents who punish kids severely end up with children who are much more aggressive than the children whose parents were lenient.

Harsh punishment tends to produce (1) aggression, (2) feeding problems.

Careful studies show that the more severely boys are punished, the more aggressively they act. (See *Patterns of Child Rearing* by Robert Sears, Eleanor Maccoby and Harry Levin.)

"It's a rare and wonderful thing when a couple celebrate their fiftieth wedding anniversary."

It's certainly wonderful, but it's far from rare: one-fifth of American marriages last over fifty years!

I know you're grunting, "The man jests!" or even "This cat is sniffing glue!" so I hasten to give you my source: *This U.S.A.: An Unexpected Family Portrait of 194,067,296 Americans*, a book of many surprises, by Ben Wattenberg and Richard Scammon, director of the U.S. Bureau of the Census from 1961 to 1965.

"Bright (gifted, creative) children tend to be sickly, lonely, emotionally unstable."

Studies by Professor Lewis M. Terman and his associates demonstrate that bright, gifted, creative children (and adults) enjoy superior health, superior social adjustment, greater success in their occupations, higher incomes and deeper, stronger emotional stability than their less lustrous fellows.

What about the many well-known geniuses who are or were dotty, loopy or certifiably *non compos mentis* (which is not Latin for "Don't let him out of sight")? Well, the famous crazies are *conspicuous* exceptions. After all, it is people who set fire to buildings who get their names in the papers, not people who don't.

My advice to embryos, after an extended study of the statistics, is this: Get born smart. The fringe benefits are sensational.

"The Bible warns us of the fires of Purgatory . . ."

Nowhere in the Bible is Purgatory mentioned. Not in the Old Testament. Not in the New.

In the third century after Christ, Origen decided that human souls must wait in a fearful place to be "purged of evil," so that, purified, they may then enter the Kingdom of Heaven. The hot spot was more formally introduced into Christian thinking in A.D. 604 by Pope Gregory the Great. His inspiration was, no doubt, the idea of the ancient Hebrews about Gehenna (from the Hebrew *Gehinom*, or "Hell"), a valley south of Jerusalem where children were sacrificed to the idol Moloch—hence the valley was said to be cursed.

Purgatory was made an official part of the Catholic hereafter in 1274, by decrees of the Council of Lyons; in 1439, at Florence; and at the Council of Trent in the 1540s.

But in 1562, the Church of England gave the back of its hand to Purgatory, which was pilloried as "vainly invented, and grounded upon no warranty of Scripture, but rather repugnant to the Word of God."

Gustav Davidson, author of the enchanting *Dictionary of Angels*, drily remarks: "We know of no angels, fair or foul, inhabiting or frequenting the place."

"The big, bad wolf . . ."

The nasty reputation of the wolf is a rank injustice. Wolves seldom, if ever, attack a human being. (I don't care *what* you learned from Little Red Riding Hood or have seen in pictures of Russian troikas pursued by slavering wolves, speeding across Siberia while babies are desperately clutched in—or thrown out of—shawls.)

". . . as promiscuous as a wolf."

Oh, if only men were as monogamous, faithful and devoted to their loved ones.

Nothing is more inaccurate than using "wolf" to describe the libidinous makers of passes at girls without glasses. Male wolves never lead a wolfess astray; in fact, wolves are stricter monogamists than men are. The male wolf is adamantly faithful for as long as his mate lives. If she dies, he goes into lifelong and celibate depression. He rarely sparks up to another female. He is also among the few mammals who devotedly help in the raising of their cubs. (For those and other vulpine tonics, browse through Pimlott and Ritter, *The World of the Wolf*.)

"At Pearl Harbor, we suffered terrible losses because the Japanese planes caught our warships inert as sitting ducks, instead of out at sea."

If ever a conclusion, drawn from undeniable facts, seems incontrovertible—surely this one does. But . . .

I have found an extraordinary letter in the *Proceedings of the United States Naval Institute* (December, 1966), a letter by Fleet Admiral Chester Nimitz, who was sent from Washington, after the catastrophe at Pearl Harbor, to become Commander-in-Chief of the Pacific Fleet. Nimitz says: "As bad as our losses were . . . they could have been devastatingly worse."

Nimitz traces the likelihood of what would have happened had the Japanese caught our ships *at sea*. Since the speed of the Japanese carrier task force was at least two knots better than the speed of our ships, and since there were six Japanese aircraft carriers waiting to drop hell on our vessels, which would have been without any air cover (or, at the very best, one carrier, the *Lexington*, which Nimitz doubted could have arrived in time); and since the powerful, modern Japanese main fleet was available in the rear for support, the following unexpected conclusions emerge:

1. The warships sunk in the shallow waters of Pearl Harbor were salvaged and repaired suprisingly soon; had they been bombed in the middle of the Pacific, they would be lying on that ocean's bottom today.

2. We lost far fewer priceless *men* at Pearl, where we saved and healed and rehabilitated so many, than we would have had our ships been sunk in mid-Pacific. "There would [also] have been fewer trained men to form the nucleus of the crews for the new ships nearing completion."

All in all, says Nimitz, "It was God's divine will that [Admiral] Kimmel did not have his Fleet at sea."

I know of no better example of an "obvious" conclusion turning, under scrutiny, into something dubious, then debatable, then dead wrong.

"Margaret Sanger was the great pioneer of birth control and women's rights."

She was great but she was not first. Before the heroic Sanger, a woman named Frances Wright lectured far and wide on birth control, the right of women to equal rights, property rights for wives, and so on. Frances

Wright died in 1852. Margaret Sanger was not born until 1883.

"The majestic, noble lion . . ."

Psst! Lions certainly look the most majestic and noble of beasts, but:

1. They are not too noble to devour the carcasses of animals killed by filthy diseases, wild dogs or despised hyenas. (Over half of lions' provender comes from these ignoble sources.)
2. Lions forget their majesty while eating their own adorable cubs, which they do, from time to time.
3. Lionesses forget maternal tradition when they breakfast on a babe—I mean, their own.
4. Lions are not noble enough to restrict their killing to the times they are hungry. Sometimes, they kill when they are so gorged they can't even nibble at their latest victim, and sometimes they break into manic orgies of slaughter.
5. Nor do lions kill as nobly and swiftly (therefore mercifully) as legend has it. They don't just jump on their victims' backs and break their necks with one decisive swing of the paw, as we have been led to believe. Oh, no. The lion sinks its teeth into the throat of a prey and slowly strangles it to death.

These surprising facts, which contradict centuries of admiring *bubbe-mysehs* about the King of the Jungle and the Lord of the Plains, were discovered by the American biologist–ethologist George Schaller of the University of Chicago. Schaller, who wrote *The Year of the Gorilla* (University of Chicago Press), an engrossing myth-smasher, spent over 120 days and nights studying lions in Tanzania's great Serengeti National Park. His report *The Serengeti Lion—A Study in Predatory-Prey Relations* is a triumph of observation, scientific method, and courage.

P.S. The lioness does 90 percent of the hunting and killing, and clearly leads and dominates the pride. The male plays second fiddle even though he is more beautiful, what with that magnificent mane. Lion society would appear to be the reverse of ours.

"There are fewer divorces among Catholics than among Protestants."

Surely *this* is true, you nod, given the Church's stern position on divorce?

The statistics undeniably show that far fewer Catholics than Protestants get divorced. But (and how large a "but" it is!) take a closer look at that word "divorced." Divorce is a legal state. You enter that state only via a court of law. Many a marriage flounders and founders and expires outside the courtrooms without legal documentation.

Now, if we add to the statistics on formal divorces the figures on marital disruptions (separations, desertion, nonsupport), which we must do to get an accurate picture of marriage stability, the picture alters dramatically. Marriages seem to *break up* just as often among Catholics as among Protestants. (Cf.: Monahan and Kephart in the *American Journal of Sociology*, March, 1954.)

Among Catholics today, about 30 percent of the marriages wind up (or will wind up) *kaput*. And that percentage is approaching the national average: one out of every three (or even 2.5) marriages in the U.S. will end up in divorce, according to *Monthly Vital Statistics*, published by the Department of Health, Education, and Welfare.

"When Galileo dropped two stones—one tiny, one large —from the Leaning Tower of Pisa, he proved that despite differences in weight, solid objects drop with equal velocity and hit the ground at the same time."

Nope. They do not—except in a vacuum.

Galileo's stones presumably hit the ground at the same time because they didn't fall far enough to be affected by air or wind resistance. Besides, stones are heavy, in proportion to their surface area, and smooth. . . .

Velocity and acceleration are powerfully influenced by air resistance. If you want to prove this to your own satisfaction, go to the Grand Canyon and simultaneously drop a feather and a cannonball. (If you can't lay your hands on a cannonball, drop a baseball, or a can of chicken gumbo soup.) You know damn well the feather won't hit bottom first.

Worse yet for popular knowledge, modern historians doubt that Galileo ever dropped *anything* from the Leaning Tower. So far as I can find out, no evidence has ever been discovered to support the celebrated story. Even in Galileo's time, the alleged experiment was a young wives' tale.

Delilah and Samson

I hate like blazes to tell you this, but Delilah never cut off Samson's mighty, might-producing hair. The lords of the Philistines told Delilah to "entice him, and see wherein his great strength lies, and by what means we may overpower him, that we may bind him to subdue him; and we will each give you eleven hundred pieces of silver."

Three times Delilah tried to lure Samson into revealing the secret of his strength, and three times Samson gave his sweetheart a different answer.

First he told her: "If they bind me with seven fresh bowstrings which have not been dried, then I shall become weak, and be like any other man." So the Philistines brought Delilah seven bowstrings which had not been dried, and she tied Samson up with them. But he snapped the tether "as a string of tow snaps when it touches the fire."

Now Delilah complained to Samson that he had mocked her and told her lies, whereupon Samson told her: "If they bind me with new ropes that have not been used, then I shall become weak and be like any other man." So Delilah tied him up with new ropes—which Samson snapped off his arms "like a thread."

For the third time, Delilah reprimanded Samson for having deceived her and asked her question. Now Samson fed her a corker: "If you weave the seven locks of my head with a web and make it tight with a pin, then I shall become weak [etc., etc.]...." So Delilah waited until her lover was sound asleep, and took seven locks of his hair and wove them into the web and made tight the bundle with a pin—but when she cried "The Philistines are upon you, Samson!" the *shtarker* woke up and easily pulled away the web, loom and pin.

And now Delilah poured out her ire: "How can you

say 'I love you'?" she cried, in woman's immemorial complaint, "when ... you have mocked me these three times, and have not told me wherein your great strength lies?" She repeated the accusation "day after day" until "his soul was vexed to death."

To put an end to her nagging, Samson blurted out the truth: "A razor has never come upon my head; for I have been a Nazarite to God from my mother's womb. If I be shaved, then my strength will leave me and [et cetra, et cetra]...."

Comes the clinching scene. Delilah told the Philistine lords that Samson had finally "told me all his mind." They gave her the money.... Delilah made Samson sleep on her knees, "and she called a man, *and had him shave off the seven locks of [Samson's] head.*" (The italics are mine.)

Delilah tormented the bald Samson, "and his strength left him ... and the Philistines gouged out his eyes, and brought him down to Gaza, and bound him with bronze fetters...."

Alors. It was a lackey, not Delilah, who shaved off Samson's locks. She was Samson's Judas—and a fink.

Of course, Samson's hair grew back. He beseeched the Lord to give him enough strength for him to pull down the pillars—while the Philistines worshipped Dagon, their god. Three thousand men and women watched and taunted Samson and made him "make sport for us."

The great house fell upon the lords and all the spectators—and Samson himself. "So the dead whom he slew at his death were more than those whom he had slain during his [whole] life."

It Just Ain't So!

All my quotations are from the Revised Standard
Version of the Holy Book. But use any edition you
want and turn to Judges 16, where the strange story
begins. You'll see that Delilah never was Samson's barber.

"One of the greatest things about America is free education."

Free to whom? Nothing comes free, really and finally.
"Free" tuition is paid by taxpayers.

What is ironic is that in our public state or city colleges, well over half the students, until recently, were the
children of middle-class, upper-middle-class and rich parents. And the poor paid taxes for those educational services—from which their children scarcely benefited
(about 5 percent). As Milton Friedman, Nobel laureate,
put it: "The people in Watts pay taxes to send the children of Beverly Hills to Berkeley."

"Edison invented the electric lightbulb . . ."

To my mind, no man ever gave more comfort to more
people on earth than Tom Edison did. But Edison did
not invent the lightbulb, on which he spent years of research and experiment. He perfected one in 1879—fifty
years after Humphrey Davy had produced an "arc
light." And in 1844, Jean Foucault had actually come up
with arc lighting for the whole Place de la Concorde.
Joseph Swan made a lightbulb (a crude thing, to be
sure) in 1860—and a carbon-filament lamp in 1878.

What Edison did was vastly improve the lightbulb by
finding a better filament.

"There's nothing in all nature so wonderful as mother love."

Perfectly right, if you don't confuse a lot of things with it. Kangaroos, fleeing some predator, sometimes heave their young right out of their pouches to lighten their load and increase their speed. Sows, of course, sometimes devour their young. Fish often eat their own eggs. And I told you about lionesses.

Are these examples too remote? Well, in one experiment, baby monkeys were reared with two "mothers"—a soft, fuzzy one made of terrycloth, and a wire one that gave milk. The monkeys preferred the soft one at all times. They used the milk-giving one only for feeding. Even worse, when startled or frightened, the little monkeys headed for the soft "mother" and ignored the milk-giving model.

MORAL: Monkeys have to have food to live, but as long as they do live, they like the soft, fuzzy feel of comfort. (See Henry Harlow's "Love in Infant Monkeys" in *Scientific American*, June, 1959.)

"When Lincoln's immortal Emancipation Proclamation freed the slaves ..."

It certainly was immortal, but it did not free a single slave.

On September 23, 1862, President Lincoln warned the Confederate states that any which did not stop rebelling and rejoin the Union before the end of the year would have all of its slaves freed, as of January 1, 1863.

Now pay attention. The proclamations of September and January were directed only against states that were at war with the Union, and did not mention slaves in those states that had remained in the Union (Maryland, Kentucky, Missouri, etc.). No Confederate states accepted Lincoln's ukase; none stopped fighting; none returned to the Union. Since Lincoln's proclamation could not be enforced, it freed no slaves. Not even in those states, fighting for the Union, which contained many slaves indeed.

Many slaves were freed, of course, before the War ended—by Union officers as they won control of Confederate territory. Such liberations preceded the Emancipation Proclamation and, later, followed it, but the relationship was merely chronological. This is not to deny that the pronouncement was highly inspirational and motivational.

The Proclamation was immensely effective in another way: by making the Civil War turn on the issue of slavery, Lincoln discouraged England and France from continuing or increasing their flow of supplies to the South.

"The enormous profits our corporations make—even after taxes—is a scandal!"

It's less of a scandal than the crazy idea that corporations make "enormous" profits.

Last year, the Opinion Research Corporation asked people to estimate how much profit American oil companies made after taxes. A majority of those polled guessed 43 percent—that is, forty-three cents for each dollar of sales.

What was the amount, say, Mobil Oil actually did earn? Under four cents.

A majority of pollees also estimated that the average

automobile company makes a profit of thirty-seven cents per buck. The Federal Trade Commission says the figure is 5.1 cents.

A majority of those polled guessed that the average manufacturer in the U.S. makes twenty-nine cents net profit each year. The actual profit last year, after taxes, was 5.4 cents. . . .

Do you want me to go on, or will you do your homework?

"Vicuña is the most expensive wool in the world."

Wrong. Vicuña costs less than qiviut. (No, that is not a typographical error; "qiviut," which you won't find in many a dictionary, happens to be one of the few English words without the obligatory *u* after the *q*.) Each pound of qiviut, which is used for making ladies' scarves, is worth about $60.

Qiviut is softer than cashmere. "Its feel," said one *maven*, "is aphrodisiacal." This is all the more astonishing when you consider that the stuff comes off the musk ox, an 800-pound creature, who resembles a buffalo—and is not really an ox, but a distant relative of the sheep.

Each bull musk ox produces about $9,000 worth of qiviut a year. *Qiviut emptor.*

"Divorce is one price of civilization, the result of the stresses and conflicts of modern living."

Would it rock you to learn that in a great many simple, agricultural societies, the divorce rate exceeds ours—and ours is high up among the nations of the West? Yale anthropologist George P. Murdock, who made extensive studies of marriage in forty primitive groups, found that in twenty-four of them the divorce rate is higher than it is in the U.S. I will not deny turning pale when I first read that.

It is wise to remember that in almost every society, there is *some* sanctioned way to end a marriage. This is true even though formal divorce, or its equivalent, is always disapproved of.

Among the forty societies Professor Murdock studied, only the Incas held a marriage forever indissoluble. Farewell, invisible Incas.

"The same people get divorced over and over."

Not in America, they don't: of all who get a divorce, 97 percent of the men and 96 percent of the women end up with only one divorce on their record.

"Birds migrate in the winter to get away from the cold to a warmer climate ..."

Thou dost err.

Birds migrate in order to eat—*i.e.*, to be where their next meal can come from. Since their food supply shrinks severely in the winter, or shrivels up entirely, the oviparous vertebrates (that's what birds are, Sam) head for the South.

"The American working class is more lusty in love, and more satisfied in sex, than the inhibited, decadent rich."

It's just the other way around. The working classes have the least free and satisfactory love-life; the upper and middle classes get far more whoopsy-do, in freer and more varied forms, in the bedrooms of our land. If you doubt me, write Prof. Lee Rainwater of Washington University in St. Louis, who made detailed studies of the sex life of American couples.

"If you're in a bad accident, you're lucky if you're thrown clear and free, out of the car, instead of being trapped inside."

If you're thrown out you'll be as dead as you are wrong. A study of 177 auto crash fatalities showed that the leading single cause of death was being thrown "free" out of a vehicle.

The best place to be in a car crash is cradled by a cushioned seat and back.

"When Julius Caesar was murdered in the Roman Forum..."

He wasn't. He took his stabbings half a mile away, in the theater which Pompey had put up. It was the most splendid building of its time, with a huge semicircle of over 17,000 seats, lovely gardens, beautiful colonnades. Attached to the gardens was the Curia, a tier of seats for the nabobs, facing an apse: it was in the apse that the celebrated statue of Pompey stood.

Since the Senate building in the Forum was being renovated, the Roman senators met in the Curia—and there great Caesar died, at the foot of Pompey's marble likeness. He suffered his pains in the apse.

"The Japanese are not original—they just copy the inventions of America and Europe."

Exactly the same charge was leveled against the English 250 years ago—and before that, Europe leaned heavily on, and borrowed breezily from, the superior know-how of the Arabs, the Chinese and India. As for the United States, we copied (mostly from the English and French) the basic idea for automobiles, movies, radio, television, radar, jet planes.

Copying is good sense—especially when you improve the technology and the product. The Japanese have done this brilliantly. They deserve considerable credit.

". . . as dangerous as a wild animal."

Tut-tut. "All wild animals are timid, sensitive and suspicious." That is the testimony of one of the most celebrated hunters in East Africa, a fearless Portuguese named Augusto Silva. Senhor Silva flatly declares that no animal ever attacks a human being except in the most exceptional circumstances.

In fact, when animals do attack one of our biped fellows, it is "for no rhyme or reason [and] should be considered as pathological abnormalities." (See James Clarke's refreshing *Man Is the Prey.*)

"Boiling lava from Vesuvius destroyed Pompeii . . ."

If it had, there would have been no Pompeii left worth excavating.

It was not lava that spelled Pompeii's doom. It was ashes and cinders.

Lethal fumes from Vesuvius killed several thousand inhabitants (and animals), who were then buried by an avalanche of ashes, a shower of cinders, and a nightmarish miscellany of volcanic *shmutz.*

When the ashes were drenched in water they hardened—forming a kind of plaster of Paris. This plaster encased Pompeii's bodies and pets and artifacts in such a way as to form a preservative mold. When, in time, the molds were chipped away, those preserved corpses were revealed that attracted tourists from all parts of the world and poured money into Italy's coffers. The last sentence is a non sequitur.

"You can't have your cake and eat it, too."

You've reversed the verbs and loused up the meaning. The saying is "You can't eat your cake and have it, too."

But then, I suppose you say, "Out one ear and in the other."

"They found his fingerprints on the gun . . ."

Police rarely, rarely find fingerprints on guns. I know that's a hard fact to swallow, but you'll have to swallow it if you're more interested in truth than illusion.

An expert of the N.Y. Police Department testified (in the trial of "Rap" Brown) that it is practically impossible to get clear, reliable fingerprints off the stock of a firearm. The expert, Sergeant William Torpey, has spent eighteen years in the city's excellent Crime Lab, has examined over 500 bullet-dispensers, and in all that time found exactly *one* useful, identifiable fingerprint.

The reasons for this astonishing fact interest me as much as the surprising fact that it is so:

a. When a gun is fired, the jolt of the concussion smears away prints that might have been clear enough to be analyzed.

b. Firearms are usually slightly oily—the better they are kept, the more oily they are. And an oily surface just won't retain crisp, sharp finger-markings: au contraire, the oily base smudges all impressions.

c. People who shoot guns usually hold them very tight—out of fear, anger or to control the aiming; but holding any lethal object that tight blurs the fine convolutions of fingermarks.

As a kicker, I give you the eye-opening datum that thumbprints were affixed to legal documents (contracts, affidavits, depositions, bills of sale) in China—over a thousand years B.C.

"Great scientists make their greatest discoveries by feats of reasoning based on experiments . . ."

Not according to many great scientists. Albert Einstein, who conducted no experiments and paid only peripheral attention to the experiments of others, said: "There is no logical way to the discovery of the elementary laws of nature. There is only the way of intuition." (See Gerald Holton's study [1969] in the *American Journal of Physics*.)

"The Mark of Cain . . ."

Oh, this one is a corker! After Cain killed Abel, the Good Book tells us, the Lord put a sign on Cain's forehead. Not one soul in a million (make it ten million) doubts that the mark of Cain was a warning to the Israelites of Cain's dire deed.

Well, it was. But that's not all it was. It was God's sign to men *not to harm Cain*, because although his sin was of the very worst, he had repented—and therefore was spared further suffering by the Lord.

What, by the way, did the mark look like? A horn.

The rabbis, by the way, argued about the meaning or message of Cain's stigma for many a generation. Some held that Cain was a leper. Others blamed him for being both a murderer and the founder of cities—cities clearly being cesspools of immorality, idolatry, atheism: Babel, Sodom, Gomorrah.

I wonder how Cain would have made out in Las Vegas.

How, by the way, did Cain die? No one knows. No one recorded it. But if you like fables, I'll give you the most imaginative one. According to legend, Cain's great-grandson Lamech went out hunting, and *his* son saw a horn in the grasses, thought it belonged to a beast, and told Lamech to let fly a stone or arrow. When they hurried to the quarry, they found that the horn belonged to Cain.

The only thing that gives me pause, in this intriguing story, is that Lamech was blind. . . . Well, maybe God guided the weapon.

"The Wars of the Roses . . ."

Ah, the white rose of York and the red rose of Lancaster. They were never used by the impassioned contestants.

It was Shakespeare who made the symbols immortal (in *Henry VI*, Part I), after the Tudors put the red and white roses in the middle of their escutcheons.

As for the designation "The Wars of the Roses," no chronicler or historian ever used it until it had been coined by Walter Scott, in 1829, in his novel *Anne of*

Geierstein. (That is not how the expression "Great Scott!" began.)

"The Bolsheviks overthrew the Kerensky government by storming the Winter Palace in Petrograd . . ."

Very dramatic, and as imbedded in history as the Boston Tea Party, but wholly wrong. The Bolsheviks did not storm the Winter Palace; they just entered it through a back door that was poorly guarded.

Three authorities confirm this: (1) John Reed, who was there, shouldered his own way through the door, and wrote *Ten Days That Shook the World*; (2) George F. Kennan, former U.S. Ambassador to the U.S.S.R., who made his own extensive investigation; (3) Norman Armour, who was at the U.S. Embassy in Petrograd at the time the Czarist regime collapsed.

"A baseball can't really curve on its path from the pitcher to the batter. The 'curve' is an optical illusion."

Wrong. The curve is not an optical illusion, delusion or *trompe l'oeil*. The baseball does take a curving path.

Before you reach for a hot pen to compose a blistering riposte, you might look up "Bernoulli" in any good encyclopedia.

The Bernoullis were a Swiss family of mathematicians, philosophers, physicists, botanists, astronomers, acousticists, naturalists and archeologists. Zero in on the one who discovered what is now known as "Bernoulli's effect." This tells us that if you throw a sphere (an orange no less than a baseball) with a spin, the spin causes the air to move *around* the sphere by friction, which is faster on one side of the globelet than the other. The air is added to the faster side from the less-fast side. Hence the sphere *must* move in the direction of the higher speed—and not in a straight line.

A baseball can be released from a pitcher's twisting fingers with enough spin to curve it as much as 1½ inches from an ordinary, unspun trajectory.

Please don't mail me indignant rejoinders. Call your local college and ask for a Professor of Physics. Or write Sandy Koufax, or Frank Aaron.

"A French doctor invented the guillotine, which was given his name."

His first name was Joseph, his middle name Ignace, his last name Guillotin (not Guillotine), and he did not invent the head-slicer that bears his name.

The guillotine was originally called a "Louison"—after a Dr. Louis who adapted the mechanism from a device long used in Italy. The reason Dr. Guillotin got into the execution business nominally is that he was a very kind-hearted physician, deputy to the Constituent Assembly in 1789, who was horrified by the instruments being used to execute or torture people. He begged the leaders of the National Assembly to make the more humane guillotine the official killing device. Until then only the nobility had the privilege of being beheaded—instead of hanged, garrotted, drawn-and-quartered, boiled or burned to death like oafish peasants or vulgar merchants.

The first guillotine in Paris was used on March 25, 1792. The first guillotinee was not a French grandee or revolutionist, but a luckless highway *bonditt.*

In time, the elevated, slanted knife was used by the government to separate the heads from the bodies of 8000 French men and women. I doubt whether 1000 of them were guilty of anything. They were victims of rumor, lies, hearsay, hysteria, the fury of the mob, the malice of officials, errors in documents, a similarity of names, and all the ghastly mistakes that accompany revolution and are inevitable in dictatorships.

Dr. Guillotin detested his bloody repute. So did his wife and children. After he died, in his bed (*not*, as legend has it, under the guillotine), in 1814, his family went to court and changed the odious name. To what? I'm asking, not answering. If you know, tell me.

"More people go crazy today, because of the terrible stresses of modern living, than went crazy a hundred years ago."

I am happy to tell you that this is not true. A careful, ingenious statistical study by Herbert Goldhamar and Andrew Marshall some years ago showed percentages of psychotics, up to age fifty, for the past hundred years in the United States.

What gives you the impression that many more people go nuts today than before is the fact that we admit many more disturbed people today to hospitals. Why? (1) Diagnoses of emotional disorders are much more frequently and quickly made than, say, in 1900. (2) Doctors think that hospitalization, new drugs and modern therapy can cure "insanity"—which they did not before. (3) People today are less likely to regard a dotty relative as simply harmless and more likely to become concerned about odd behavior—so they take the dotty one to the nearest psychotherapist or clinic. (4) Fewer people lovingly keep daffy relatives in the attic than they used to do. There are also fewer attics; young marrieds buy or build houses where storage space is in the garage, which is a good place to keep a cuckoo clock, but not a cuckoo aunt who has you in her will.

All in all, the presumed increase in lunacy only testifies to refinements in diagnosis and the general mores; it does not show an actual increase in the number of nuts per capita. Not that that number is low enough to reassure anyone. Just listen to some of the late talk shows on television, or some of the debates in Congress, or some of the utopian palaver of warm-hearted, soft-headed Doers of Good.

Sometimes I mourn for a republic in which inmates are more muddle-headed than outmates.

"George Eastman took the first true photograph."

Nyet. Eastman invented a machine, in 1884, which could make photographic paper (i.e., paper impregnated with certain chemicals) in long rolls. This made photography cheap and popular, and accounted for the success of the Brownie box camera.

The first true photograph was made in 1824, in Châlons-sur-Marne, by Joseph Niepce, yet.

"Americans are the hardest-working people in the world."

Not according to the figures. Hungarians work a fifty-hour week, and the French, who enjoy a reputation for sitting in cafés all day drinking, gabbing and goofing off, work longer and harder than Americans do. These facts come from a survey (by the National Statistics Institute in Paris and the Social Sciences Center of Vienna) of how people in ten countries spend their time.

While we're on the French, we may as well spike another canard, if that's what you do to canards. Housewives behind the Iron Curtain spend much more time preparing meals for their husbands than French women do! To the surprise of the survey conductors (and me), it turns out that French wives use more prepared, supermarket dishes than anyone dreamed.

Further, every Sunday the housewives of most nations celebrate by dropping their weekday routines, but on Sundays the French housewife spends the same amount of time on the same chores as she does during the week.

"Mammals can't fly . . ."

Bats are mammals, and they fly. Bats are the only mammals who have developed this ethereal ability. ("Flying squirrels" don't really fly; they leap—then float downward.)

Digression: The baseball bat is not derived, etymologically, from any object designed to strike bats. The baseball "bat" comes from the Irish *bata* or *batlet*, meaning a wooden stick with which to beat washed clothes. (In nonelectrified communities, women still pound clothes on rocks and stones along a river—to beat the water out of them, I suppose.)

"One of the shrewdest Yankee sayings is 'Tell it to the Marines!' "

I do not think Walter Scott was a Yankee—and he's

the one who coined the brisk retort. Scott's whole comment runs: "Tell that to the Marines—the sailors won't believe it."

The Scotsman was referring to British sailors and marines. The American usage is opposite: It suggests that you and I, the Knights of Pythias, the B'nai B'rith and the Loyal Order of Elks believe some tall yarn or another that our heroic Halls of Montezumans wouldn't swallow come hell or high water. The Marines are justly famed for not swallowing whilst immersed in high waters.

"Adolescence is a time of great conflict and emotional upheaval."

In America and Europe it certainly is, but not where adolescence is thought of as being devoid of conflict, and where cohabitation among adolescents is taken for granted. A sensitive, persuasive picture of that kind of adolescence is, of course, Margaret Mead's classic *Coming of Age in Samoa*.

This, of course, gives you no clue about my feelings about the comparative psychological advantages of repression as against expression in our ambivalent society. The question is always: How *much* freedom, at which age, for which child, in what circumstances, with what attitude, with what degree of parental approval or noncommitment?

Even if we admit that virginity is no longer the *sine qua non* of virtue, and that "making out" seems as common today as making Brownies was yesterday, "that ole debbil" sex goes right on weaving his snares and hang-ups.

It Just Ain't So!

"Suicide occurs most frequently among the overworked, the skinny, the inhabitants of cold, gloomy climates and in the depressing winter months."

Nope.

Overwork causes far fewer suicides than no work or underwork.

More fat people kill themselves than do skinny people.

More suicides take place in May than in December or March or any other dreary month.

One of the highest suicide rates in the world is to be found in San Diego, where, the Chamber of Commerce tells me, it's bright, clear and sunny 300 out of 365 days of the year. (That's not why people kill themselves there, either).

As for poverty, low standard of living, poor food, endemic disease—Egypt has one of the lowest suicide rates in the world.

"People in Scandinavia commit suicide more often than people in other European nations because the highly advanced social welfare and security systems make people bored—removing the invaluable challenges, competition, initiative and excitement of life."

Then why were suicide rates in Sweden, Denmark (and Switzerland) so high in the eighteenth and nineteenth centuries, long before these countries had far-reaching welfare states?

Research by Professor Herbert Hendin of Columbia offers us some eye-opening facts. Professor Hendin interviewed a goodly number of Scandinavians who had tried to commit suicide, and he concludes that the most frequent cause for their desperation was not boredom but intolerable strain. The Swedes and Danes live on a ferocious competitive level, it seems, at home. At school, on the playgrounds, under universal military service, they are molded to push themselves to the farthest point of their capacity. This applies to the social whirl as well. To be outclassed, or not invited to homes you would like to be invited to, imposes a severe strain and festering humiliation.

God knows that the plays and novels of Scandinavian countries are shot through with gloom; any reader of Ibsen knows how inhibiting were the mores in that part of the world.

Some psychoanalysts are coming around to the idea that there are more (and more complicated) neuroses among the presumably "phlegmatic" Nordics of the North than among the oral, narcissistic, expressive extroverts of the Mediterranean littoral.

Several years ago interviewers asked Swedes: "What are you afraid of?"

"Loneliness" was a common answer. "We are not good at making friends. Our families are small. Old people live alone."

A teacher said, "Two-thirds of our young people feel they have failed. And today, they can't blame the rich, or the capitalist system, or the social system. They can only feel inferior. This creates a fierce kind of alienation. In fact, ours is a harsher class system today than the old one, in which there were divisions by wealth."

Another teacher, commenting on the singularly high

standard of living, ruefully concluded, "Maybe some hardships will help us become human."

Norway, emphatically a welfare state, has a very low suicide rate (7 per 100,000). And in the U.S., suicides seem to have declined after the advent of the paternalistic New Deal.

"What about Denmark?" comes a voice from the gallery. That's a tantalizing question. Denmark, a welfare state in spades, has a simply *whopping* suicide rate: 20 to 30 per 100,000. But wait. The suicide rate among Danes has been high for a century and *declined* after the adoption of social-welfare legislation; and the decline was most pronounced among those over sixty-five—the group most heavily benefited by paternalism.

Suicide, like life, is woven of innumerable, subtle skeins. (For an interesting and fresh look, see Maurice Farber's *A Theory of Suicide.*)

"People who live a simple life go crazy less often than people who live under great tension."

"People in quiet, rural areas crack up less often than people forced to live in the jangling jungle of our cities."

Both statements—so plausible, so "obvious," so stoutly and widely accepted—are wrong. If you doubt me, peek into J. A. Clausen's "The Sociology of Mental Illness," in *Sociology Today*, edited by R. K. Merton.

"Divorce is hell on children."

Probably—but no more, and possibly a good deal less, than the continued hostility, squabbling and rage which a child witnesses between parents chained to each other by legal bondage.

The data show that marital discord is more likely to produce disturbed or "problem" children than does divorce, or the death of a parent.

When things reach the stage where divorce has become thinkable, continued marriage-with-hate is worse for the children. (Evidence? See William J. Goodes' "Family Disorganization," in Merton and Nisbet's *Contemporary Social Problems*.)

"Having children reduces the chances—and the numbers —of divorce."

Only in the sweet imagination of those who have not examined the figures. Children play only a small and incidental role in preventing divorces or maintaining marriage-on-the-rocks. (See Berelson and Steiner's definitive *Human Behavior: An Inventory of Scientific Findings*.)

"We would greatly help poor and underdeveloped nations if we increased the amount of food we send them."

If we send food to poor nations, except during an emergency drought or famine, we make their long-range plight worse. Huge shipments of free food decrease the price of farm products in the recipient nations: This depresses their farming (and their farmers), drives agricultural workers into indigence and out of farm work and lowers the amount of food grown in the future. And farming, please remember, is the major industry in those lands.

In India, the government leaned on huge wheat hand-outs from us—and let their agriculture decline while the giddy bureaucracy poured money into more prestigious (and economically unsound) projects. The same sequence of events has occurred in other countries helped/harmed by American generosity. Lavish aid encouraged governments to build roads, airports, steel mills and flashy, chauvinistic but economically idiotic monuments to the government in power.

A shattering book by Professor Theodore Schultz, the distinguished agricultural economist, demonstrates that if the United States doubled its farm output and handed out all of our excess foodstuffs to underveloped nations, we would (for the reasons above) make the plight of the poor and underprivileged around the globe worse than it now is.

I say nothing about how our aid reduces the foreign exchange which is gravely needed by impecunious nations—to buy machinery, power plants, etc., or to hire technicians and specialists from abroad.

"Cockroaches love dirt."

Not according to roachologists. The favorite food of cockroaches (*Dictyoptera*), of which there are 3500 different species, is not dirt. Nor is it honey, sugar, spices, frankincense or myrrh.

The delicacy that drives *Dictyoptera* daffy with delight is (of all things!) soap.

"A typical Horatio Alger rags-to-riches story . . ."

As a boy I gobbled up the Alger pitch of virtue thrice-rewarded. In my memory, Alger's poor newsboys and

shoeshine gamins became captains of fortune soon after
they returned a lost wallet to a banker, or helped a shab-
bily dressed old lady across the street (she was really a
millionairess) or stopped a runaway horse that was carrying the boss' frantic daughter to a broken neck.

Imagine my dismay, therefore, when a cynical friend
told me that *not one of Alger's noble characters ever
won fame or millions.* "I have made a study of the entire
corpus of Alger's fiction," the leering gent said, "and not
one of Horatio's stout lads ever got more than a raise—
of five or ten bucks a week."

I have not slept well ever since.

"Yellow fever is the bane of life in the tropics."

I would be the last to deny it—but down the years
yellow fever, with its fierce temperature, jaundice, retch-
ing and vomiting, has killed millions upon millions of the
inhabitants of France, England, Italy, Greece and other
untropical zones. Yellow fever is a dreadful scourge in
African lands far from the tropics.

Yellow fever is caused by a virus transmitted by the
bite of certain mosquitoes, especially the breed called
Aëdes aegypti. Such mosquitoes have infected and mowed
down the inhabitants of Philadelphia, Boston and cool
towns in South America. (The Philadelphia and Boston
nightmares came from mosquitoes, bred on shipboard in
their harbors, which infested the population during hot
summer days.)

Contrary to popular misconception, yellow fever does
not rage in the Far East, nor even in hapless India—
albeit the particular mosquitoes which carry the virus
are found in abundance there. Yellow fever was eradi-

cated in many Latin American lands by 1940, but *Aëdes aegypti* can be found today in Texas (sorry, pardner) and some southeastern states.

In terms of insect-borne diseases, incidentally, the safest big country in the world is Ireland, where nothing much more lethal cavorts than the bumblebee. Between the dazzling colleens and Irish blarney, the absence of snakes, Yellow Jack, and pornography, Ireland is a dandy place to visit.

P.S. The cheerful psychopath who rules benighted Uganda, Colonel Amin, created as his country's highest military decoration The Order of the Mosquito, because it was the mosquito (says Amin) that persuaded England to relinquish sovereignty over Uganda.

"As civilization spreads in this cruel world, as men become more literate, more advanced, less ignorant, less primitive—they treat their children ever so much more kindly."

What an uplifting thought! What a tribute to progress! And what a piece of falsification.

The styptic truth, recorded by anthropologists, goes just the other way: By and large, primitive people are kinder, more lenient, more patient, more affectionate to their young than are the parental products of technologically advanced societies—including the disciples of Dr. Spock, who is nowhere as "permissive" as his misreaders make him.

Primitive peoples do not wean their babies so early, do not potty-train them as rigorously, are far less inhibited about s-e-x, and respond to their children with less ambivalence, guilt or severity of demand than we do.

Please don't flood me with hair-raising tales about the harsh Mundugamor or the savage Gitchie-Goomee; I began the comparisons by saying "by and large"—and I mean a large "by" and an even larger "large."

Since nothing will stop some patriots from smothering me with protests and contumely, I cite *Child Training and Personality: A Cross-Cultural Study* by John W. Whiting and Irwin L. Child, and *Patterns of Child Rearing* by Robert L. Sears, *et al.*

"England and America got rich through imperialism—by exploiting their colonies or backward countries..."

Is there any article of faith so dear to the heart of the liberal? Does anyone deny the viciousness of capitalist nations? When I was at college, a standard textbook, *Imperialism*, by Parker Moon, professor at Columbia, taught us all how greedy trade and vile profits "follow the flag."

But Paul Samuelson of M.I.T., Nobel laureate, author of the most influential textbook on economics of recent times, an unimpeachable liberal, recently wrote:

> I do not know whether on balance Britain benefitted from owning India. The computation is a difficult one. Certainly the Dutch were not crippled by losing Indonesia or the Belgians by losing the Congo. France is better off without her empire in North Africa and Indochina. . . .
>
> Just as there are few indispensable men, there are few indispensable nations. Were the world to lack the resources of the Indian peninsula, and also its hundreds of millions of people, would Western living standards be lower? White South

Africans probably enjoy a higher standard of comfort because each lives on the toil of 7 black men. But is it likely that the top ⅔rds of our people would be impoverished if the poorer ⅓—black or white—did not exist?

What remains then of the concept of exploitation? ... Let me quote Paul A. Machiavelli: "The poor have property rights in the rich." This is a fact, not a target.

"The experts who predict population growth ..."

No one is an expert in predicting population growth: what authorities on population do is make *projections* from existing data. I learned this from one of the world's leading analysts of population figures, Professor Philip M. Hauser.

The difference between predicting and projecting is subtle: to project is to forecast what will happen if birth and mortality rates continue to be what we know them to be at the time the projection is made. "Absolutely no one anticipated the remarkable control of mortality, and the remarkable decreases in the death rate, which have been achieved," says Professor Hauser.

I should add that over a decade ago Professor Hauser said that for the next decade the world will "just have more people,—and more people of low quality. The outlook seems dismal." It is.

"The Robber Barons were scoundrels who exploited the people until Congress passed laws which prevented such depredations."

Matthew Josephson popularized the "Robber Barons" sobriquet, and his book of that name has become some sort of classic. Josephson electrified and outraged us with indisputable data about these shameless buccaneers of capitalism, who lined their pockets by picking ours.

Today, historians with no unground axes or bleeding hearts reveal that these predators pulled off their most scandalous capers only through collusion with, and crucial assistance from, agencies of government. Public officials were the ones who created and protected the wolves.

Railroads, for instance, got stupendous subsidies from federal or state laws, then farmed out the costly construction or expansion to phony subcontractors: themselves. The notorious Erie Gang (Gould, Fisk, Drew) made their bonanzas through secret stock manipulations only because New York's legislature was controlled by the public servants whom the villains bribed. The Californians known as the Big Four (Stanford, Hopkins, Crocker, Huntington) operated through shmeered puppets in Sacramento: the Central Pacific Railroad became one of the most brazen flimflams in our history—because the Robber Barons were given a government monopoly on certain rail routes. At one point you could send freight to San Francisco by *ship*, all the way around South America, for much less than the legally protected Central Pacific charged to haul it.

To nail the case down, compare the records of competitive and "unprotected" railroads. Vanderbilt and Hill and the railroads they ran without any government payola or monopoly were more profitable to their stockholders and much cheaper to shippers than was the Central Pacific. The Eastern empire-builders did not steal a dime from the taxpayers—in "subsidies."

You will find a slew of similarly startling revelations

in *The Incredible Bread Machine,* a little book written by six young researchers at the World Research Institute in San Diego. I beg all true believers in public ownership or federal regulations to read it. The book takes ninety minutes to scan but ninety hours to ponder. The 192 pages send fresh breezes through "progressive" but erroneous clichés about our wicked capitalist system.

But the Robber Baron story continues to be taught in our colleges just as Matthew Josephson originally (and innocently) told it.

"The motor that lifts our elevator . . ."

Your elevator car is not lifted by a motor. Every elevator car has a counterweight which, when released, just falls in the shaft—and that raises the car.

The drive motor only lifts the rather small difference in weight between a fully loaded car and its counterweight.

The mechanisms of elevator ascent and descent mesmerize some people; they are not of the slightest interest to me.

"Business executives who drive themselves too hard get more heart attacks than less-ambitious men who take it easy."

A five-year study of over 270,000 men shows that hard-driving business executives are *not* more susceptible to heart disease. What seems more important than the way men work are such factors as heredity, body build, obesity, exercise, smoking, social background, educational level. Coronary disease may, in fact, be determined long before a man sets foot on the lowest rung of the well-known Ladder to Success.

What especially interested me about the research findings was that even eager-beaver workmen, the ones most often promoted, praised and raised, showed no more coronary problems than guys of the same age who took everything nice and easy.

Caution: All this pertains to heart problems. It would not surprise me to learn that career-crazy, high-strung, ambitious men are plagued by hives, ulcers and insomnia—even while their lazier, fatter, somniacal friends drop like flies in front of television sets.

Anyway, I just don't understand why people put so high a premium on longevity. Just visit any home for the aged.

" 'Hobson's choice' means no choice."

It means "Take it or leave it," which surely is a choice! (When Henry Ford was urged to make his standard black Model-T in other colors, he replied, "All right. What shade of black do they want?")

Thomas Hobson was a stable owner in the seventeenth century. The reason his humble name became part of a celebrated catch phrase is that Hobson made it a rule that anyone coming to his stable to rent a horse had to take the horse at the head of the line. Hobson refused to waste time satisfying his clients' preference for "that chestnut mare in the middle" or "the white-nosed horse near the end." Hobson's choice came down to this: "Take the first horse or skidoo."

You'd be surprised by the number of well-educated

souls who believe that "Hobson's choice" means "six of one or a half-dozen of the other."

Misnomers

English muffins are an American invention. They were totally unknown in England until recently, when supermarkets, another American contribution to culture, began to import them.

"Irish stew" is a meaningless phrase in Ireland.

Danish pastry, which sells better than hotcakes in every coffee shop in the U.S., is known as "Vienna bread" in Denmark.

Croissants, that flaky triumph of Parisian breakfasts, were first rolled in—Vienna. The shape derives from a tantalizing tidbit of history: The Turks, who were given to invading Central Europe with ferocity, particularly enjoyed besieging Vienna. During the siege of Wien in 1683, a pastrymaker expressed his hatred for the Turks by beating his dough into thin layers of dough (36 layers!) which he formed into the shape of a crescent, the sign of Islam. The Viennese, a people gifted in gossip, flirtation and that scorn for time known as *schlamperei*, seized upon the croissant as a masterpiece of symbolic contempt, and gobbled up the Turkish emblem with patriotic delight. "Since we could not beat them, we ate them."

Russian dressing is a taste thrill you can travel from Murmansk to Yalta without once finding on or near a salad. The *tovarischti* never heard of the culinary frill.

French dressing. Your guess is right: the name is wrong. Oil and vinegar are used for salads all over

France, of course, but if you call it "French dressing" the natives grow restless and look as if you're trying to con them into a game of "Knock-knock." To say "French dressing" in Paris is like saying "the wet Seine" or "the musical Opèra." I do not advise it.

Jerusalem artichokes have not the slightest connection with Jerusalem, nor a choking man named Arty. The legume got its moniker from the fouled-up pronunciation of the Italian word for sunflower: *girasole*, which the Jerusalem artichoke sort of resembles.

Pizzas were a pasta-with-ornaments unknown (or very rarely found) in Italy until American tourists demanded them. The American passion for pizzas was bred in the Italian quarter of New York and spread like wildfire throughout the United States. Today, pizzas perfume the piazzas of Rome.

Spanish rice, if ordered in even the best *restaurantes* of Madrid, will get a puzzled expression. Spaniards never heard of the stuff.

Vichysoisse, that unique and delicious soup, does not come from Vichy. Vichysoisse was the contribution to soupdom of the chef at the old Ritz-Carlton in New York. True, he used the recipe of his mother, who had fed him hot potato soup at night and the cold remainder for lunch next day.

Welsh rarebit is more than a rare bit in even the finest castles in Wales. Where the melted-cheese-with-beer-on-toast originated I have no idea. Nor do I care for it.

Turkeys do not come from Turkey; they were brought *to* Turkey (and Europe) from, of all places, Mexico, by Spanish and English conquerors. The English called the gobblers turkeys on the mistaken assumption that they were close kin to the guinea hen of Eastern (therefore Turkish) Europe.

Turkish baths are not of Turkish ancestry.

Valencia oranges. A spy long in my service reports that he could not find a single orange of this identity in Valencia.

Malaga grapes. My spy's wife scoured Malaga in vain for them.

Oranges should be called "noranges," because the name goes back to the Latin *aurum* ("gold"). The "n" got lost in the French separation of the definite article, *une.* Spaniards say *naranja,* Persians say *narang,* and the Arabs say *naranj.*

Little Bastards

India ink. It never came from India, but from China.

Honeysuckle. This lovely name is rooted in the belief that bees like to suck honey from the fragrant flowers of the twined, climbing vine we all know and love. But honeysuckle is not of the slightest interest to bees, who are not fooled by language. It is clover flowers which are rich in honey—and *they*, originally, were called "honeysuckle" (from the Anglo-Saxon *hunigsuce: hunig,* meaning honey, and *sucan,* "to suck").

Bees still suck clover with ill-concealed scorn for humans who can't tell the difference between a low-growing leguminous plant and a high-growing social climber.

Jordan almonds. They come from Spain. Their only relationship to Jordan is spurious: as a corruption of the French *jardin.*

Whalebone. This part of a whale's upper jaw, used by

Yankee sailors for the carvings called scrimshaw, contains no bone at all: It is a tough "strainer" membrane, which filters the algae and water out of the inedible stuff whales can't help swallowing when they forage for more succulent fare.

Finally:

"The biggest industry in the United States is the automobile industry."

Not by a long shot. Neither is the production of steel, iron, detergents, dentifrices or deodorizers.

The biggest industry in the United States, in terms of money spent or people employed, is Education—bigger even than everything involved in Defense. Last year we shelled out $120 *billion* on education, as against $87 billion for defense. (See HEW's 225-page report.) Schooling, from kindergarten to Ph.D.s, also employs the most skilled professional personnel to be found in any industry.

Our education Gargantua, one of the true wonders of history, also fills the minds of students with enough false, inaccurate, foolish, deluded or delirious poppycock to fill a thousand books such as the one you are holding in your hands. Let it fall now, and go to sleep.

3.
QUIZ
ON QUOTES
or
"Well,
I'll Be Damned!"

"No man is lonely
while eating spaghetti
—it takes so much attention."

—*Christopher Morley*

Take a pencil. Smile at the simplicity of this quiz as you tick off your answers to the questions below. Score ten points for each correct answer.

QUESTION: *Who originated each of the following sayings?*

1. **"Ask not what your country can do for you—ask what you can do for your country."**

    _____ John Fitzgerald Kennedy
    _____ Benedict Arnold
    _____ Charlie Brown

2. **"Go west, young man."**

    _____ Henny Youngman
    _____ Mae West
    _____ Horace Greeley

3. **"I do not agree with a word you say, but will defend with my life your right to say it."**

    _____ Jimmy Carter
    _____ Voltaire
    _____ Mary Tyler Moore

4. "... the iron curtain. ..."

_____ Jacqueline Onassis
_____ Muhammad Ali
_____ Winston Churchill

5. "The only thing we have to fear is fear itself."

_____ Joe Namath
_____ Franklin D. Roosevelt
_____ Barbra Streisand

6. "All's well that ends well."

_____ Vergil
_____ Shakespeare
_____ Casey Stengel

7. "Everybody talks about the weather, but nobody does anything about it."

_____ Mark Twain
_____ Samuel L. Clemens
_____ Tex Antoine

8. "... the New Deal. ..."

_____ a Las Vegas blackjack dealer
_____ Groucho Marx
_____ Franklin D. Roosevelt

9. "... a chicken in every pot. ..."

_____ Herbert Hoover
_____ Colonel ("Finger-lickin' good") Sanders
_____ Jackie Gleason

10. "England is a nation of shopkeepers."

_____ Karl Marx
_____ Peter the Great
_____ Bismarck

11. "God is on the side of the stronger battalions."

_____ Clausewitz
_____ Napoleon
_____ Adolf Hitler

12. "Give every man the benefit of the doubt."

_____ Catherine the Great
_____ Oliver Wendell Holmes, Jr.
_____ Oliver Cromwell

13. "A nation's greatest treasure is its scholars."

_____ Socrates
_____ Mme. de Staël
_____ Ralph Waldo Emerson

14. "Idle young men make miserable old men."

_____ Will Rogers
_____ Benjamin Franklin
_____ Montaigne

15. "I have brought you peace with honor."

_____ Neville Chamberlain
_____ Ho Chi Minh
_____ Chou En-lai

16. "Experience is the name we give our mistakes."

_____ Bernard Shaw
_____ Dorothy Parker
_____ Oscar Wilde

17. "Alas, poor Yorick, I knew him well."

_____ the gravedigger in *Hamlet*
_____ Horatio
_____ Hamlet

18. "... laissez-faire...."

_____ David Ricardo
_____ Adam Smith
_____ Meyer Rothschild

19. "... the four freedoms...."

_____ Abraham Lincoln
_____ Justice Louis Brandeis
_____ Franklin D. Roosevelt

20. "When good Americans die, they go to Paris."

_____ Maurice Chevalier
_____ Oscar Wilde
_____ Benjamin Franklin

21. "... the lunatic fringe...."

_____ H. L. Mencken
_____ Disraeli
_____ Schopenhauer

22. "One-third of our nation is ill-fed, ill-housed, ill-clad."

_____ Seneca
_____ Franklin D. Roosevelt
_____ Robert La Follette

23. "She would rather light a candle than curse the darkness."

_____ Eleanor Roosevelt
_____ Helen Keller
_____ Adlai Stevenson

24. "A dream uninterpreted is like a letter unopened."

_____ C. J. Jung
_____ Aristotle
_____ Sigmund Freud

25. ". . . survival of the fittest."

_____ Attila the Hun
_____ Charles Darwin
_____ Emperor Hirohito

26. ". . . the Great Society. . . ."

_____ Homer
_____ Lyndon B. Johnson
_____ George Washington

27. "The difficult takes a while, the impossible a little longer."

_____ Slogan in World War II
_____ Howard Hughes
_____ Thomas Edison

28. "Nothing fails like success."

_____ Igor Stravinsky
_____ La Rochefoucauld
_____ Oscar Wilde

29. "... government of the people, by the people, for the people."

_____ Thomas Paine
_____ Jean-Jacques Rousseau
_____ Abraham Lincoln

30. "Any man who hates dogs and babies can't be all bad."

_____ Bob Hope
_____ W. C. Fields
_____ Marquis de Sade

O.K. Wasn't that easy? Now let's check your answers. Perhaps you had better swallow a tranquilizer first—because every single check you made is wrong. That's right, wrong.

1. "Ask not what your country can do for you...."

These were Cicero's words, roughly, when he addressed the Roman Senate in his inaugural address, in 63 B.C., on the day he became Consul.

Oh, sure, John F. Kennedy used the memorable line in his inaugural in 1961; but remember: my question was "Who *originated* the saying?"

2. "Go west, young man."

This one was coined by John L. Soule in the Terre Haute *Express* in 1851. In fact, when Horace Greeley later uttered the provocative line, he said he was quoting John Babson (!) Soule. (How John L. Soule became John Babson Soule, I do not know.)

"Go west, young man" became one of the most revered slogans in the American credo, and Greeley often protested that it was not he but Soule who had coined the clarion injunction. It did no good.

(I also admire Greeley because of his nifty illustration of false inference: "I never said all Democrats were saloon-keepers. I said that all saloon-keepers are Democrats.")

3. "I do not agree with a word you say, but will defend with my life your right to say it."

Voltaire? Nearly everyone thinks so. Year after year, this majestic line appeared, credited to Voltaire, above the *Letters to the Editor* column of the New York *Herald-Tribune*. It had first appeared in the U.S., with the same accreditation, on the masthead of an Ohio paper whose name I cannot locate.

The odd thing is that no one has ever found the noble statement anywhere in Voltaire's works—and experts by the score have read themselves blind trying to run down the line.

The best they were able to come up with was the dismaying discovery that in 1906 a British biographer named Evelyn B. Hall, writing under the pseudonym "S. G. Tallentyre," used the epigram in her book, *The Friends of Voltaire*. She used it as if she was quoting from Voltaire's *Essay on Tolerance*. But the aphorism does not appear in Voltaire's essay. And on September 1, 1935, in a letter to *The New York Times*, Evelyn Hall/

Tallentyre declared that she had only tried to "para-phrase" Voltaire's central ideas and never dreamed that her formulation would be taken literally.

Bergen Evans, in his huge, erudite *Dictionary of Quotations*, says Tallentyre "made up" the epigram. And Ashley Montagu and Edward Darling, in their darling *The Prevalence of Nonsense*, flatly declare that Voltaire never said it at all.

Now, hold everything. I am happy to tell all you bated-breathers that I have uncovered the following sentence, written by Voltaire on February 6, 1770, to Abbé A. M. de Riche:

> "... I detest what you write, but I would give
> my life to make it possible for you to continue
> to write."

That's close enough, for my money. The popular Hall/Tallentyre wording is far better, of course, and you have my permission to use it from now on with aplomb, given M. Voltaire's letter to the Abbé de Riche.

4. "... the iron curtain...."

Oh, how I hate, hate, hate to disillusion you. The incomparable Winston Churchill, one of my shining heroes, rocked the world at Fulton, Missouri, on May 5, 1946, in a speech which contained that unforgettable passage:

> "From Stettin in the Baltic to Trieste in the
> Adriatic an iron curtain has descended across the
> continent."

But a year earlier, a Reuters dispatch in the Manchester *Guardian* (February 23, 1945) quoted the unspeakable Joseph Goebbels' warning, in *Das Reich*, that

> "the whole of east and southeastern Europe . . . [might] come under Russian occupation. Behind an iron curtain, mass butcheries would begin."

If Goebbels had anything it was *chutzpah*.

But the foaming demagogue did not suspect that the Talmud says: "Nor can an iron wall [or curtain] separate Israel from God" [*Pesachim*, 85:2]. Nor that one of the prayers Jews recite on the seventh day of Sukkoth (Tabernacles) ends with a plea that God "remove the iron curtain [our sins] that comes between us and You." Nor that H. G. Wells used the phrase in 1904, in his *The Food of the Gods*:

> "Beyond the Vistula River, a curtain falls which makes it hard to discover what is happening inside the Russian empire."

The decisive adjective "iron" is missing—but it appears with all its power in several accounts of what the Queen of Belgium, born a princess of Bavaria, said in August, 1914:

> "This is the end! Between the Germans and me there is now a bloody iron curtain—which has fallen forever."

And in 1915, George Crile, in *A Mechanistic View of War and Peace*, called France, if you please, "a nation with . . . an iron curtain at its frontier."

Reader: This page is dull. Skip it—and half of the next page. Unless, of course, you are as compulsive as I am.

In 1918, Vasily Rozanov published *The Apocalypse of Our Time*, in which you will find these words:

> "With a roar and a rumble, an Iron Curtain is descending on Russian history."

And in 1920, Ethel Snowden (no relation to the photographer) wrote a book called *Through Bolshevik Russia* in which she exclaimed:

> "We were behind the iron curtain at last!"

And if that isn't enough, I must tell you that in 1921, one P. Mohr contributed an article to a journal entitled *Information About Eastern Questions*, in which this prophetic phrase appears:

> "Bolshevik Russia lay concealed behind an iron curtain."

Finally, to return to Winston Churchill, about a year *before* his speech in Fulton, he sent a top-secret telegram to President Truman (May 12, 1945) deploring conditions on the Eastern (Russian) front the very week after the Nazis had surrendered:

> "An iron curtain is drawn down over their front. We do not know what is going on behind... The whole of the region east of the line Lubeck–Trieste–Corfu will soon be completely in their hands... and then the curtain will descend."

On October 21, 1945, six months before Churchill's speech in Fulton, St. Vincent Troubridge wrote (in London's *Sunday Empire News*):

"There is an iron curtain across Europe."

I hasten to wave aside your admiration for my scholarship: An AP dispatch from Moscow in 1946 first alerted me to Goebbels' use of the phrase; a letter from Vienna to *Encounter*, that priceless journal I always read with avidity, a letter written by Friedrich Henn, of whom I know nothing, meticulously documented much of the data I have passed on here.

I will blush modestly if you care to congratulate me for the quotations from the Talmud and the Sukkoth prayer.

5. "The only thing we have to fear is fear itself."

This electrifying sentence was indeed spoken by Franklin D. Roosevelt on March 4, 1933, in his inaugural address. But in Thoreau's *Journal*, the entry for September 7, 1851, reads:

"Nothing is so much to be feared as fear."

And the incomparable Montaigne said, "The thing of which I have most fear is fear." And Francis Bacon has a similar phrase in one of his essays. And I am bracing myself for a storm of indignant letters from FDR's fans.

6. "All's well that ends well."

Shakespeare, of *course*, wrote a play so named, and used the line in the play. But "All's well that ends well" was a well-known saying, steeped in folk wisdom, long before Will worked for the Globe Theatre. You will find the exact saying, described as one "popular in the marketplace," in the Talmud (*Baba Kamma*, 92b, 93a). (It doesn't matter which edition or translation of the Talmud you use: all use the same paragraph and subparagraph numbering.)

7. "Everybody talks about the weather, but nobody does anything about it."

Everybody on earth seems to think Mark Twain said that, but it was Charles Dudley Warner, editor of the Hartford *Courant*, who really wrote the delightful quip —in an unsigned editorial in 1890.

What Mark Twain said about all the credit he got for what he didn't say I am still trying to find out.

8. "... the New Deal...."

Franklin D. Roosevelt, accepting the nomination at the Democratic convention in Chicago in 1932, said: "I pledge you—I pledge myself, to a new deal for the American people."

But back in 1919, no less a figure than Lloyd George had campaigned on this slogan: "A New Deal for Everyone." And in 1871, Carl Schurz talked of "the prospect of 'a new deal'" (his quotes).

The most jolting joker of all, to me, is that just a few hours *before* FDR's acceptance speech, one John McDuffie of Alabama orated to the same convention: "There is a demand for a new deal in the management of the affairs of the American people." No one noticed.

9. ". . . a chicken in every pot. . . ."

Bless my soul, this phrase was immortalized in Al Smith's biting attacks on President Herbert Hoover for having uttered the promise during the Depression of 1932. But poor Hoover had not *once* let those fricasséed words cross his lips! The phrase appeared in a Republican campaign leaflet, and Mr. Hoover squirmed for it ever after.

Who *first* said "a chicken in every pot"? William Safire credits France's king Henry IV: "I wish there were no peasant in all my realm so poor as not to have a chicken in his pot every Sunday."

What are the odds that someone said it earlier?

10. "England is a nation of shopkeepers."

Sure, Napoleon said it. The catch is that he was quoting—Adam Smith's *Wealth of Nations:*

> "To found a great empire for the sole purpose of raising customers [is] unfit for a nation of shopkeepers, but extremely fit for a nation whose government is influenced by shopkeepers."

11. "God is on the side of the stronger battalions."

It is perfectly true that Napoleon said this. But so did Voltaire, in a letter on February 6, 1770. And so did the Comte de Bussy, in 1677, writing to the Comte de Limoges. And before *them*, Tacitus wrote *Deos tortioribus adesse* ("The Gods are on the side of the strongest") in his *History* (Book IV, par. 17).

12. "Give every man the benefit of the doubt."

Scratch Catherine the Great (she had ladies of the court test the sexual prowess of young men before she allowed them in the royal hay). Scratch Oliver Wendell Holmes. Scratch Cromwell.

"Give every man the benefit of the doubt" comes from the Mishnah: *Pirke Abot* ("Sayings of the Fathers"), 1:6.

13. "A nation's greatest treasure is its scholars."

You may be sure Socrates, de Staël and Emerson agreed with this old Chinese proverb.

14. "Idle young men make miserable old men."

Neither Will Rogers nor Ben Franklin nor Montaigne coined this one. Who did, I do not know. Then how can I say that neither Rogers, Franklin nor Montaigne did? Because I found it in a collection of old, old folk sayings dear to the hearts of the Maori of New Zealand.

I'm confident that Will, Ben and Monty were not Maoris.

15. "I have brought you peace with honor."

History will not forget that ghastly day in October, 1938, when Prime Minister Neville Chamberlain returned from his sellout of Czechoslovakia at Munich and came down the ramp of his plane, in London's airport, proudly waving a piece of paper.

Chamberlain, a quite stupid and self-righteous moralist, waved the paper before a battalion of microphones and newsreel cameras and announced that he had persuaded Adolf Hitler to sign a statement ("Here is Chancellor Hitler's signature!") which declared that, having Czechoslovakia handed to him on a plate—territory, people, munitions plants, a tough army, tanks, and a superb air force—all for nothing except bluster, blackmail and a temper tantrum, the Führer now declared himself as happy as could be, and had graciously promised that he had "no further territorial claims," dreams or desires in Europe. "I bring you peace," crowed Chamberlain. "Peace for our time! A peace with honour!"

Less than a year later, Hitler crossed the Polish frontier and launched World War II.

Neville Chamberlain, the mustached merchant from Birmingham, did not know that the most memorable (and ludicrous) phrase of his career was but an echo of the words ascribed to Theobald of Champagne (c. 1135), or to Disraeli who, in 1878, had returned from his parlays with Bismarck at the Congress of Berlin to tell the British people, from an upper window at 10 Downing Street: "We have brought you back peace—but a peace, I hope, with honor."

Disraeli, a consummate statesman, diplomat, writer and wit, had the good sense to say "I hope." His peace did last—until 1914.

16. "Experience is the name we give our mistakes."

Alas for Oscar Wilde, to whom this flashing insight is usually attributed. Alas for Bernard Shaw or G. K. Chesterton, too. Or for Sydney Smith or Samuel Butler or François Arouet (Voltaire), who are also credited.

"Experience is the name we give our mistakes" is an old folk saying of the Jews.

17. "Alas, poor Yorick, I knew him well."

This quote is not from *Hamlet*. It is not even in *Hamlet*. Hamlet did not say it. Neither did the grave-digger—nor Ophelia, Polonius or Yorick's uncle in Elsinore.

What Hamlet did say was: "Alas, poor Yorick. I knew him, Horatio."

How so widespread a misconception has come down the centuries, and why Horatio's name was dropped and "well" was added, I cannot figure out.

18. "...laissez-faire...."

The apotheosis of the laissez-faire system of economics is, of course, Adam Smith's monumental *Wealth of Nations*. But nowhere in the text does Smith use the phrase. It was coined by the French economist Jean Claude de Gournay (1712–1759). The complete phrasing he used was "...*laissez faire, laissez passer.*" Let it not pass.

19. "...the four freedoms...."

This one may rouse you to a rampaging rage. It is true that on January 6, 1941, President Franklin Roosevelt, in a message to Congress, proclaimed the hallowed words: "...we look forward to a world founded upon four essential human freedoms" (freedom of speech, freedom of worship, freedom from want, freedom from fear).

The bug in this noble ointment (I wish it was not so) is that "the four freedoms" appeared earlier in the pages of one of the most awful, turgid, evil books ever written: *Mein Kampf*, by Adolf Hitler. May both rot in hell.

20. "When good Americans die, they go to Paris."

Show me the college major in English who doesn't know that this zinger decorates Oscar Wilde's *Lady Windemere's Fan*. It does. *But* it is preceded by the precautionary words, "They say, Lady Windemere, that when good Americans [etc. . . .]."

To keep the credits clean, I remind you that the delightful animadversion may be found in Oliver Wendell Holmes, Sr.'s *The Autocrat of the Breakfast Table*, which was published forty-odd years before Oscar Wilde's pastiche was performed. And to keep my conscience clear, I murmur: And Dr. Holmes, mind you, was quoting Thomas Appleton.

21. ". . . the lunatic fringe. . . ."

This bonny *bon mot* was originated by Theodore Roosevelt (no less), in a letter to Henry Cabot Lodge, in 1913, four years after The Big Grin left the White House.

22. "One-third of our nation is ill-fed, ill-housed, ill-clad."

Except for the last word, which he gave as "ill-clothed," this ringing cry of protest was uttered by H. G. Wells, in *The Day of the Comet*.

I'm not saying that Franklin D. Roosevelt or his

speechwriters (Samuel Rosenman, Robert Sherwood, *et alii*) stole the potent phrasing. I'm not even sure FDR and his advisors read the Wells book. All I'm saying is that the line appeared in print long before the President so effectively delivered it.

23. "She would rather light a candle than curse the darkness."

Adlai Stevenson made this moving eulogy to Eleanor Roosevelt after her death: "She knew it was better to light a candle than curse the darkness." That lovely line went around the world. Did Mr. Stevenson know he was quoting, or did he think he had made up the brocard?

The first time I ever saw "It is better to light a candle than curse the darkness" was on the letterhead of the Christophers. And when I met Father Keller, that good man who heads the Christophers, I expressed my admiration for the sentiment. He exclaimed, "Oh, goodness! That wasn't original with me. I heard it *years* ago."

Neither Father Keller nor I know where the line was born. (If any reader does, please write.)

24. "A dream uninterpreted is like a letter unopened."

I don't blame you if you put a checkmark after Freud or Jung or Aristotle. I, however, ran across it in *Yebamoth* (118b), which happens to be one of the sixty-odd little books or tractates in the Babylonian Talmud. You can read it in English, in the twelve volume translation published by Soncino Press and available from Ktav Publishing House in New York.

25. "... survival of the fittest."

Darwin greatly admired the phrase, which he took from Herbert Spencer in 1859 and used to historic effect. Darwin wrote, "I have called this principle... natural selection, but the expression often used by Mr. Herbert Spencer, of the survival of the fittest, is more accurate" (*Origin of Species*, Book III, 1859).

Then Darwin learned that the wording had been suggested earlier, by one William Wells in 1813, and another, Patrick Matthew, in 1831.

26. "... the Great Society...."

Lyndon B. Johnson loved the phrase. It was his attempt to resurrect and extend "the New Deal." It is also the name of a splendid book by Graham Wallas, published in 1914.

27. "The difficult takes a while, the impossible a little longer."

This witticism was plastered all over the offices, hangars, shops and barracks of our armed forces around the globe during World War II. (So did the sign FOOD WILL WIN THE WAR—under which an unknown GI printed: "But how can we get the Krauts over here to eat it?")

Be that (or those) as it may, the invigorating slogan about the difficult and the impossible seems to have been coined by Chaim Weizmann, first president of Israel. You read it on the title page of his wife's memoirs, *The Impossible Takes Longer*.

28. "Nothing fails like success."

Could any epigram sound more distinctively Oscar Wildeian? No. But G. K. Chesterton seems to have

coined it, in that marvelous parade of paradoxes he called
Heretics.

**29. "... government of the people, by the people, for
the people."**

Of course, Abe Lincoln wrote and spoke the immortal
triad in the Gettysburg Address.

But Theodore Parker, addressing the Boston Anti-
Slavery Society in 1854, used those words. And on January 26, 1830, Daniel Webster told the Senate that our
government was "made for the people, made by the people, and [is] answerable to the people."

I have for years believed that in the preface to his
translation of the Bible, John Wycliffe, "The Morning
Star of the Reformation," wrote in 1382: "This Bible is
for the government of the people, by the people, and for
the people." I believe it because of a note in my research
files, but I have not been able to prove it. Help, help.

**30. "Any man who hates dogs and babies can't be all
bad."**

Sure, sure, I know: Umpteen anthologies of quotations credit this to W. C. Fields. But he did not say it. He
may have said, "A woman drove me to drink, and I
never even wrote to thank her," or "How do I like children? Boiled," or "Never give a sucker an even break."
But he did *not* come up with "Any man who hates dogs
and babies can't be all bad." The line was uttered *about*
Fields....

The place was Hollywood. The time: 1939. I was
working on a solemn sociological (or was it anthropolog-
ical?) study of the movie colony. One day, to my sur-

prise, I received a telegram from the Masquers' Club, inviting me to be their guest at a banquet in honor of W. C. Fields.

I was delighted. I was transported. I revered Mr. Fields as the funniest misanthrope our land ever produced. And I knew that the Masquer dinners of homage were in fact "roasts" in which celebrated wits eviscerated the guest of honor with sparkling insults, scintillating persiflage and steamy boudoir revelations which, if uttered on any other occasion, could provide an airtight case for a lawsuit worth millions in damages for character assassination. I accepted the invitation with alacrity.

I appeared at the Masquers with a wide grin and anticipatory chuckles. The lobby was packed with moviedom elite: stars, producers, directors, writers. All male, all famous, all treating me, as I circulated amongst them, the way princes of the blood treat a peasant with anemia. I might have been made of glass, so easily did the glances of the celebrated go right through me. But I did not mind. I was very young, and felt lucky to be a guest on Parnassus. My heart thumped faster as I recognized noble Spencer Tracy, great Goldwyn, wonderful William Wyler, incomparable Ben Hecht. And was that Errol *Flynn* holding court in the corner? James Cagney with admirers near the clock? John Wayne? John Huston? John Garfield? Humphrey *Bogart*?! I do not know. I was not sure, to tell you the truth, because I was so excited that my vision and my imagination were playing leapfrog.

Suddenly I heard my name blaring, over and over, from loudspeakers, and an agitated voice pleading that I report to the desk "at *once!*" My heart sank. Had one

of my loved ones fallen into the La Brea tarpits in search
of a neglected dinosaur? Had my best researcher just
been crushed to death in a stampede outside the Brown
Derby?

I ploughed through the glittering assemblage to the
distant desk, where I was told by an icy factotum that I
was "damn late" for one who would be seated "*on the
dais!*" A majordomo swiftly (and sourly) led me back-
stage. There I beheld Mr. Fields, already red-nosed from
fiery waters, surrounded by illustrious roasters: Groucho
Marx, Bob Hope, Jack Benny, George Burns, Edgar
Bergen, Milton Berle. . . . It was they, I assure you, in the
flesh.

"Time to line up!" called a Praetorian guard.

A hotel Hannibal began to recite name after hallowed
name. Mine, unhallowed, was last.

"Pro*ceed* to the dais!" blared another *macher*. Someone flung heavy red draperies aside.

As we marched through the opening and across the
stage, the glittering audience rose to its feet, applauding
—applauding Marx, Benny, Hope, reaching a crescendo
for Fields, hailing Berle, Bergen, Burns—until I appeared,
last, certainly least, pale, brave, anonymous. The applause
seeped away like sand in a net of gauze. One pair of
hands clapped valiantly—those of someone from MGM,
I assume, who must have thought me Louis B. Mayer's
nephew from Kankakee. Amidst the anticlimax of my re-
ception, we all sat down to break bread. . . .

The dinner was excellent, the wines ambrosial, the
brandy and cigars sublime. Then William Collier, Sr.,
rose to conduct the festivities. He received an ovation,
which he deserved. A renowned M.C. and wit, he orated

a barrage of dazzling, scathing yet affectionate ribs about our putative guest of honor. The audience roared in counterpoint. And to each barbed line, Mr. Fields responded with an evil grin, a leering grunt and another sip of alcoholic disdain.

I was beside myself. Such polished harpoons, such reinforcing laughter, such mordant expressions from W. C. Fields, crowning Collier's insults with Fieldian bravado.

Mr. Collier completed his backhanded eulogy. A tornado of applause. Then the masterful M.C. proclaimed: "Our first speaker to 'honor' Bill Fields is. . ." (he consulted his prep sheet and, there is no denying it, winced) "Dr. Leo Boston—no, I guess it's *Rosten.*"

It would be wrong to say that I could not believe my ears; the full measure of my horror lay in the fact that I did. I sat paralyzed. This could not be. It was a dream. It was a nightmare. I blinked, to hasten awakening. I wondered what had happened to my pillow. It took the elbow of Red Skelton, jabbing into my ribs, to propel me to my feet.

The "applause" which had greeted Mr. Collier's garbled recitation of my name would not have awakened a mouse. Now, my erectness and visibility compounded my shame, for the faces of that auditorium broke into frowns of confusion and the many mouths uttered murmurs seeking enlightenment. But there I was, standing, numb, dumb, unknown, staring into a star-filled sea of faces staring glumly at me. I prayed for a trap door to open beneath me, or for lightning to strike me dead. Neither happened. Instead, I heard George Burns' hoarse *sotto voce:* "Say *some*thin'!" with unmistakable disgust.

I gulped—then someone who was hiding in my throat

uttered these words: "The only thing I can say about Mr. W. C. Fields, whom I have admired since the day he advanced upon Baby LeRoy with an icepick, is this: Any man who hates dogs and babies can't be all bad."

The appearance of Mae West in a G-string would not have produced a more explosive cachinnation. The laughter was so uproarious, the ovation so deafening, the belly-heavings and table-slapping and shoulder-punchings so vigorous, that I cleverly collapsed onto my chair.

I scarcely remember the rest of that historic night—except that the jokes and gags and needlings of Mr. Fields (who by now resembled a benign Caligula) put all previous celebrity "roasts" to shame.

The next morning, the local papers led off their stories about the banquet with my ad lib. The AP and UP flung my remark around the world. CBS and BBC featured the quip on radio. Overnight, I was an international wit.

Alas, God put bitters in the wine of my enflatterment; for ever since then, "Any man who hates dogs and babies can't be all bad" has been credited to—W. C. Fields. Hardly a week passes in which I do not run across some reference to "Fields's immortal crack." But it was mine. Mine, I tell you, *mine!*

Now reread the subtitle of this chapter. And stop *frowning.*

4.
FAN
MAIL

"I would rather go to bed
with Lillian Russell
stark naked than with Ulysses S. Grant
in full military regalia."

—*Mark Twain*

I have been pruning my correspondence file for the past year. It is a mortuary chore. For it depresses me to see with what patience and kindliness I answered all my mail—not only letters from the bright and worthy, but kooky inquiries from fans who seem to consider me the son of "Dear Abby" and the *World Almanac*.

I don't know why people think that a writer is omniscient (or even niscient): a seer, sage, psychiatrist, astrologer, biochemist and expert on bearded irises rolled into one; but readers do—they certainly do. I suppose it's because laymen attribute magic to print. They confuse a skill (writing) with a state (wisdom): so they (the readers) write the damndest requests to them (the scriveners).

Every author learns, sooner or later, that some of his most ecstatic admirers are types who fall into the category, made famous in Otto Knädelschlinger's definitive *Metatarsal Fetichism*, called "nuts." Oh, I do get some exceptionally intelligent letters, but my prose seems to exert a magnetic attraction upon distraught pinball addicts, epileptic masseuses and near-sighted bowlers. I especially seem to rile recidivist peatmoss thieves, who sit around waiting for Lefty to publish something that will heat up their gonads, whereupon they leap to their desks and let fly.

How does one answer loony letters? H. L. Mencken, whose hate mail has never been equaled for vituperative juices, used to answer all *billets*, however nasty, with a postcard on which was printed:

> Dear Sir or Madam:
> You may be right.
> Yours,
> *H. L. Mencken*

This gave some of his correspondents apoplexy; others' hair began to fall out.

I regard Mencken as one of our national treasures, a polemical genius worth pairing with Swift and the least-appreciated humorist in American letters. But I dance to a different flautist. I find it hard to castrate anyone, even with words.

I follow the Good Book's injunction that a soft answer turneth away wrath, so my replies to correspondents, even those snippy or scurrilous, are like flies in September: lazy and low-keyed. I send the most insipid amenities through the U.S. mails, trying to set my *enragé* an example of dignity, tolerance and goodwill to all men.

Why do I do this? Because I am a coward. I just can't churn up the courage to ignore disgusting correspondents entirely or flay their hides with the silky whip of an Oscar Wilde, the thunderous scorn of a Samuel Johnson, the blistering bile of Don Rickles—instead of with a craven courtesy that may endear me to my pen pals but draws a rasp across my self-esteem.

Every so often I rebel against my milksoppery, and in my mind compose the most searing, soul-satisfying replies imaginable. (I generally do this on afternoon walks around the neighborhood, where my sotto voce cacklings and chortlings cause pedestrians to hurry to the other side of the street. Matrons often do so in the middle of a block, which violates a city ordinance.)

My soliloquous revenge is a harmless catharsis, God knows; and letting off steam that way enables me to regain that sweetness of character, that unflinching devotion to the Golden Rule which leads me to answer letters in the ensuing months with benevolent hypocrisy.

Of course, I pay a price for my shameless piety. Every New Year's Eve, when I review the past year's highlights and lowlights, I plunge into a murky depression. The best way to cure a murky depression is to retire to a murky cell and console yourself with recollections of all the good deeds you tossed around during the preceding annum. This I faithfully do. But my sins make a shambles of my virtue.

There are two kinds of sins, as any secondhand dealer in morals will tell you: sins of omission and sins of commission. For instance, you *commit* a sin when you throw a teetotaler into a beer vat; you *omit* a sin if you don't pull him out. I don't know how to make that any clearer.

The sins I committed last year are not likely to make Beelzebub lick his chops: They were trivial falls from grace, like telling the personality girl who telephoned breathlessly "You have just won a free lesson at Yolanda Slotnick's Dance Studio!" that I had lost a leg in a PTA brawl. Or filching the stamp off a return envelope for a no-money-down offer of color slides of Mount Rushmore. Or telling a moist-eyed sophomore from Radcliffe that in my opinion the only way Rod McKuen can be ranked with Shakespeare is if he recites his poems to the tune of "Avon Calling."

My sins of omission were no more juicy: the five bucks I forgot to send the Anti-Hominy Grits League; the leaky faucet I did not repair for three days during the water shortage in July; the chocolate fudge sundae cum whipped cream I ate in August. (A Jesuit might label that a sin of commission, but I list it in the opposite department because I omitted the nuts that came at no extra charge.)

Well, after I have chastised myself to a frazzle for such surrenders to evil, I rally my synapses and remind myself that there is hope for even the most egregious sinner. My Daddy told me that the redemption ticket-window is never closed; I can repent, recant and pledge my soul to abounding virtue in the year ahead. That's when I sit down and draw up my New Year's resolutions. They would bring joy to the heart of St. Theresa. Consider this year's fervent promises:

1. Write Mother more often.
2. Find out what "polyunsaturated" means.
3. Read *Everything You Ever Wanted to Know about Sex, but Were Afraid to Ask*; then send it to Xaviera Hollander.
4. Ask her to send me samples of *The Happy Hooker*.

5. Do not strike, maim or otherwise injure people who babble about the courageous "message" of such fraudulent movies as *Last Tango in Paris, Easy Rider, The Trial of Billy Jack* or *Seven Beauties.*

There is one resolution I did not make, admirable though it is, because I just am not man enough to go through with it:

6. Answer stupid letters with forthright scorn and not in cowardly, soft-answer-turneth-away-wrath prose, viz:

Dear Mrs. Creepover:
Thank you for your extremely interesting and informative letter. I do not myself happen to believe that buttermilk will discolor your earlobes, but I fully appreciate the sincerity of those who, like yourself. . . .

Here, in a rite of purgation, are excerpts from some of the loopier letters that crossed my desk last year, plus the answers I wish I had had the gumption to send back, were I a man and not a *mouche:*

"Who wrote 'The Battle Hymn of the Republic'?"

I did.

"I heard someone say that you once won the Noble Prize. Is that true?"

Yes. I won the Noble Prize in 1968 for my invention of an index to Webster's Dictionary.

The Noble medal is made of the finest alpaca, and is about the size of a kettledrum. Mine is inscribed:

> *TO A NOBLE FELLOW*
> from
> *Morris R. Noble*

Morris R. Noble, who died of prolonged inhaling, was an immigrant from the Bronx who founded the Hug-Tite Girdle Corporation. It was his lifelong interest in girdles that made him set up a foundation.

Incidentally, Noble's prizes are always awarded in Torquemada's Spa in the Catskills, and not in Stockholm, Sweden, which is why I never go there.

"Is it true that Spiro Agnew, who is my idle, changed his last name from Agronsky?"

No. Spiro Agnew, who is my idle, too, changed his first name from Shapiro.

"What is meant by the expression 'the Minor Leagues' that I constantly read about on sport pages?"

In the minor leagues all players must be under twenty-one. They have to show their birth certificates to the umpire at the start of each game.

When players reach their twenty-first birthday, they are moved to what is called the "major" leagues, whether they want to go or not. The old Brooklyn Dodgers could not make up their minds whether they were majors or minors; that is why they moved to Los Angeles, which shelters many fugitives of the same species.

"Who wrote the words for that grand old favorite 'Shuffle Off to Buffalo'?"

I did. Buffalo Bill wrote the music.

"Who was the first police commissioner of Kalamazoo, Michigan?"

I'm glad you asked.

"Do you believe in interracial marriage?"

Absolutely not.
Intermarriage between the male and female races is the sole cause of humanity's problems.

"... the Secret Meaning of Isaiah 8:14 makes it ABSOLUTELY PLAIN the world will END August 3 at 10:30 P.M.!!! What do you say to that?"

Isaiah man like you is crocked.

"Do you know the name of a good book on basket-weaving?"

Frequently.

"If I go to the Argentine, will the moon still look like our man in the moon?"

No. He'll be standing on his head. That alone is worth the price of a night-coach flight to Buenos Aires. *Bon voyage.*

"Why do we add, subtract, multiply etc., 'backward'—I mean, from right to left, instead of from left to right, the way we write?"

Because we inherited our numbers and arithmetic from the Arabs. In Arabic, as in Hebrew, texts read, as they are written, from right to left. Arithmetical reckonings were and are done the same way.

If this upsets you, use a mirror.

"What's the funniest story you know about hotels?"

The one about the Southern belle who, on her first trip to the Big City, entered the hotel elevator and, en route to Room 1263, brightly pressed buttons 12, 6 and 3.

"What's the meaning of 'Fifteen men on a dead man's chest'...?"

"... yo-ho-ho and a bottle of rum."

One of the curious things about nursery rhymes and famous ditties (such as the pirate chantey above, from *Treasure Island*) is that they contain so much that would puzzle children if they ever thought about them. They don't. Kids just love the cadence, and cryptic phrases only enhance their pleasure.

Fifteen men sitting on one dead man's chest, if you visualize it, is absurd. It should please you no end, therefore, to learn that there is a tiny Caribbean island that was known to the buccaneers from England, Spain, France, Portugal as "The Dead Man's Chest." It is shaped in a way the outlaws of the sea never forgot: like a huge chest on a prone human male.

Disgruntled carpers may cry, "The 'dead man's chest'

was a *treasure* chest!" *I* am gruntled enough to prefer the island explanation. *That* chest was big enough for fifteen desperadoes to sit on. Yo-ho-ho and plenty of room.

"While you were a teacher of English, what rules can you give people like I to avoid making bad mistakes?"

I have twenty-five foolproof rules, even for good mistakes. But I did not formulate my admonitions *while* I was teaching English; I set down my Twenty-five Tips after I escaped.

1. Correct speling is a Must.
2. "Just between you and I" is a Mustn't. It's as much of a mustn't as "They telephoned she."
3. Be sure to never split an infinitive.
4. Being human, don't dangle with participles: "Running for the bus, a taxi hit my uncle." The cab driver was daydreaming about his dependent clauses.
5. The subtle difference between "teach" and "learn" should learn you to pay attention: Teachers don't have to pay attention, so they don't learn; they just teach.
6. When studying grammar, a spiral notebook of well-lined pages are useful. This shows that subjects and verbs are enemies.
7. Don't never use no double negative. Triple negative are even worst.
8. Always make a pronoun agree with their referent.
9. Beware of the "them–those" trap. For instance, don't write "Them apples are rotten" if they are not.

10. Many people just *love* to use commas, which are not necessary. For instance, "She ate, the fool" is a comment. "She ate the fool" is correct, if you are describing a cannibal.

11. One of the trickiest points in punctuation is to use apostrophe's correctly. They are as sensitive as measle's.

12. Never use "real" when you mean "very." Therefore: "She is real stupid" shows that you are very stupid. This point is real important.

13. Adjectives are not adverbs. Write careful. I know that's hardly.

14. Question marks can be dynamite. Use them carefully. "You sure are pretty?" means you are not sure I am pretty. That is an insult.

15. Many a student is undone by "who" and "whom." Remember George Ade's remark: " 'Whom are you?' she asked, for she had gone to night school."

16. Avoid the excessive use of exclamation points!!!! It is silly to write, "Yesterday, I woke up!!!" because that suggests that today you did not, which is probably true.

17. When you want to say something that indicates anyone, or all of us, the pronoun "one" is better than "he" or "she." Fats Waller put it neatly: "One never knows, do one?"

18. Observe the difference between "don't" and "doesn't." It's shocking to hear so many high-school graduates say "He don't care." What they mean, or course, is "I don't care." Their grades proved it.

19. Never write "heighth" or "weighth." They just are not righth.
20. If you write "Who's hand is stroking my thigh?" you'll never know who's pulling whose leg. Such information can be valuable.
21. "Irregardless" is not in the dictionary. "Hopefully" is—and I hope to God you never use it.
22. Don't use "neither" when you mean "either." Either use "neither" correctly or don't use it at all. And don't use "either" if you mean "ether" neither.
23. Guard against foolish repetitions. This here rule is especially important for new beginners.
24. A real booby trap to avoid is "when"—especially when a sentence like "I do not deny I wasn't afraid" occurs when you mean "I won't deny I *was* afraid." Most writers are, so they master syntax, which is the only tax that doesn't cost money.
25. Don't forget the crucial difference between "lie" and "lay":

    a. The former takes no object ("I lie in bed") but the latter must ("Lay that pistol down, Mother").
    b. "To lie" means expressing something not true; "to lay" means expressing something more urgent.

Okay? Now, memorize these laws and be sure to reread anything you write in the future to make sure you don't accidentally any words out.

"People like I" should avoid writing to people like me.

"I heard a TV highbrow say that Einstein proved that space is curved. That drives me nuts. Can you explain 'Space is curved'?"

Easily. It all depends on what you mean by "is."

"Who holds the Olympic record for the fifty-yard breast stroke?"

I do. I hold the breast-stroke record for all the other distances, too.

"Do you know a cure for hiccups?"

Certainly.

"Can you answer the puzzler: 'What happens when an irresistible force meets an immovable object'?"

An inconceivable solution. (I wish this was original.)

"Which one thing most inspires you to write?"

The Bureau of Internal Revenue.

"Who discovered the Sea of Cortez?"

I did.

"We just bought a French poodle for our daughter, who wants to call him Amen-hotep. Con you give us an idea about what to do? We think Amen-hotep is a peculiar name for a poodle."

So do I. Amen-hotep is even a peculiar name for a praying mantis. Besides, he was not French; he was an Egyptian gambler, addicted to playing pharaoh.

Tell your daughter she must learn to respect other people's hang-ups. A poodle named Amen-hotep is likely to think he is a mummy and may spend all his time lying on the floor with his paws folded across his chest. Dogs who lie on their back all day are no fun to throw sticks at.

People should be very careful about the names they give pets. I know an oculist who rashly called his pet canary Florence. He thought this would make Florence sing like a nightingale. He was fit to be tied when Florence began to sing "Ol' Man River" in a deep bass.

The oculist should have realized that the male ego (be he canary or hoot owl) hates nothing more than being called Florence. And *no* one I ever heard of can bring off "Ol' Man River" in the soprano register. The last time this was tried was by a celebrated *sopranistin* in Salzburg named Paula Tarsus, during on *Oktoberfestgezangsvereinfeierungspiel*. She had hardly reached "*Er anplanzt nicht potatoes*" before she was driven off the stage by an irate barrage of *pfennings* and *tomaten*.

"What is your favorite tongue-twister—like 'She sells sea-shells at the sea-shore'?"

My favorite idiocy of this genre is not a tongue-twister but a word maze:

"If this doctor doctors that doctor, does the doctor who doctors the doctor doctor the doctor the way the doctor he is doctoring doctors doctors or does the doctor doctor the doctor the way a doctor who only doctors doctors does?"

To get to mere tongue-twisters, this one, which I elaborated for my children, is the slipperiest:

"She sells sea-shells and shell-fish at the sea-shore but she's so selfish selling shell-fish that she seldom sells sea-shells, so who shall sell sea-shells she seldom sells selfishly selling shell-fish?"

Now I lie down with a cold towel on my forehead. That's what my kids did, too.

"Do you happen to know why Chinese doctors always keep ivory statuettes of women in their office?"

Man, do I! Only last week I was obliged to visit a new ear-nose-and-throat doctor (he started rubbing his hands the minute I entered his office). As we sat down, I noticed on his desk an ivory statuette of a nude female about eight inches high. Ivory midgets have always exercised a disturbing effect on me, so I probably shifted about somewhat more than the ordinary patient who is about to have his nose, throat and ears explored by a Marco Polo of otolaryngology.

"Bet you don't know what *that* is," grinned Dr. Genzel, with a grin so wide I understood (from his tonsils) why he had chosen his moist medical specialty.

"Marlene Moskowitz."

"That is *not* Marlene Moskowitz," he snapped. "That happens to be a Chinese Doctor's Lady."

I would not gratify his ego by asking why a sinologist, who had no doubt become interested in knickknacks while still in alimentary school, kept a statue of a naked broad on his desk. So he donned an annoyed expression (the one M.D.s use whenever a patient refuses to feel better after taking the latest miracle drug, a mixture of sesame seeds and liver extract from Bolivian mules) and proceeded to enlighten me:

It seems that in old China, no proper lady would dream of undressing before a man, even her honorable physician. So Chinese medicos used what has, since the Mink Dynasty, been known as a "doctor's lady," such as the one that had caught my eye. Fastidious female patients, on being questioned by their healers, would point daintily to one or another spot on the ivory, indicating the zone where their complaint was lodged. Chinese doctors made their diagnoses from that. They lacked patience.

"How good is a bird's eyesight?"

No bird, however old or decrepit, has ever been seen wearing bifocals. Most breeds have flattish eyeballs with very large retinas. Any camera nut can tell you that eyes like that act as wide-angle lenses, covering a great deal of territory with unusual "depth of focus."

Birds of prey (this has nothing to do with church attendance) have rounder, tabular eyes, which cover less ground but see much farther—and in incredible detail.

So you see that "as keen as a hawk" is no idle metaphor: It's a simile.

"Why are there so many rats in slums?"

Not only because of the presence of garbage, but because of the absence of snakes. Call your local Herpetological Society.

"I see you wrote a book about malapropisms. What are your favorite ten?"

1. "God rest ye, Jerry Mandelbaum . . ."
2. Radium was discovered by Madman Curry.
3. Antidotes are what you take to kill dotes.
4. "I pledge allegiance to the flag and to the republic for Richard Stands."
5. Cervantes' masterpiece is *Don Coyote*.
6. "Our father who art in heaven,
   Hallowe'en Thy name . . ."
7. Joan of Arc was the wife of Noah.
8. It's been a long time since I haven't seen you.
9. "Gladly, the cross-eyed bear . . ."
10. An oral contract isn't worth the paper it's written on.

And that does not include the immortal child's version of a Christmas carol: "Hark, the angel Harold sings. . . ."

"Have you ever heard of Mattress Flatteners? Where can I buy one? I have a mattress so lumpy that when I sleep on it I feel like I'm on a roller coaster."

Am I glad you asked that!

Mattress Flatteners are proud professionals who walk around the streets of Bombay twanging melodies of identification on long wooden instruments with vibrating strings. (What difference does it make if I don't know the instruments' names?) These hardy Hindus spend their hours of employment pounding lumps out of mattresses. For all I know, they use bats, laths, planks, poles or petrified pillars of salt. Or they jump up and down like vertical dervishes. One way or another, they smash mattress protuberances out of existence.

I don't think you can buy a Mattress Flattener. I suggest you buy a new mattress. Get your lumps later.

"Did you ever know Aimee Semple McPherson?"

Not that I know of. But I did enjoy her evangelical shenanigans. What I most admire is her faith: She was buried with a telephone beside her.

"Do birds yawn?"

So far as I know (which isn't very far into birddom), the parrot actually yawns. I think that's because parrots get bored by the oddballs who keep nagging them to say, "Polly wants a cracker." How would *you* feel if that was the only sentence you could get your owner to understand?

"What's the most peculiar wedding custom you ever heard of?"

Well, this one's not the most *peculiar*, necessarily, but it's certainly the one I remember with the most delight: In sturdy Vermont, in the early days of its sturdy settlement by sturdy settlers, the bride would stand in a closet, naked, thrusting her arm through a little hole sawn out of the closet door. Thus deployed she would make her wedding vows, and thus deployed did she receive the wedding ring on her disembodied finger. The preacher and the groom stood outside the closed door of the closet, of course. They couldn't glimpse the nude bride through the hole.

Why this peculiar mummery? Because through this gambit the groom demonstrated that he was not marrying the girl for filthy lucre or "earthly possessions." Tchk, tchk.

"Is there a cure for the common cold?"

Alleged cures for colds are as numerous as ants in the Antilles:

In Devon I was told that you must take a hair from the cougher's head, place it between two slices of bread (buttered is more efficacious than nonbuttered), give this singular sandwich to your dog and intone: "May you be sick and I recover." That's a helluva way to treat faithful Fido.

In parts of Cornwall, the locals shave the patient's head and hang all of the hairs on a bush. Since birds use hair for lining their nests, they are supposed to swoop down and carry the hairs—and the cough—away.

In parts of France, superstitious farmers boil three snails in barley water. This will cure a cold—unless the sick one knows about it. "You must be very careful to boil the snails in secret!"

Most cures for colds are just as sensible and effective as these. Try one of them. If the cold doesn't disappear, perhaps you will. I can hardly wait.

"How prolific are termites?"

I think you mean "How fecund."

A queen termite can live for fifty years, and can produce 500,000,000 eggs. (Don't ask me who counted.)

One African female of the species lays 43,000 eggs *per*

diem, without a penny's compensation from the government.

"Why do we say 'mad as a March hare'?"

Because hares go wild with passion every March. That month is rutting time.

"Rutting time" does not refer to the minutes spent in running up and down ruts. It means the cyclical period when lust runs riot, and sexual excitement and reproductive banging reach their peaks.

"Who was the first man to put sardines in a can?"

I knew some smart alec would try to trip me up with a tacky question like that.

Well, it was not a Norwegian, nor a Portuguese, nor a New Englander. It was a Frenchman named Blanchard. I vouch for that.

"Do the Danes really wrap a cow in an overcoat and take him for a walk?"

What do you mean "really"? Either they do or they don't wrap a cow in an overcoat and take him for a walk.

It is true that in Denmark the natives used to do that. I don't think they do so today. Of course, once a Dane reads this item and wants to get his name on the AP wire. . . .

"How did animals ever get the names we call them by?"

One of the tidier things man has done is to give names to things: birds, beasts, insects, fishes. This was not easy. An ichthyologist, for instance, can't just take a pencil and clipboard and dive down to a blunt-nosed flounder, say, and ask: "Excuse me, fish: I am taking a poll for the U.S. Census Bureau. What is your name, please?"

The men in charge of fish-naming *did* try this system at first, but they got fouled up something terrible because the fish had all seen *To Tell the Truth*, so every fish, when asked "What is your name, please?," gave the same answer: "Glp."

This led the ichthyologists, who have an unshakable faith in research data, to conclude that *all* fish are named "Glp." But when they fed this into a computer and asked for its opinion, quick as a flash came the answer: "No!" When a computer answers "No!" instead of just flipping its disks, you can be sure something important has happened in the world of science.

The same thing happened to the zoologists, who were assigned to name animals. *Every single specimen of a species interviewed gave the same name.* Every dog, for instance, said his name was "Bark"; every cat, "Meow"; every cow, "Moo," and so on.

For a long time, during the Idiopathic Era, people went around calling every dog "Bark" and no one minded, but when men began to move out to the suburbs and called their dogs in from the street to give them their vitamin-enriched chopped liver, any one man's call of "Here, Bark! Here, Bark, Bark, Bark!" brought every dog in the neighborhood to his door. They came like lemmings, and many died of overeating.

Things couldn't go on this way, so dogologists decided to name each *breed*, once and for all. They gave many a dog a bad name, like "Schnauzer." Anyone knows that if you call a sensitive dog a Schnauzer, he will develop post-nasal drip.

According to legend, when Noah was loading the Ark, God appointed an angel, whose good sense He especially trusted, to name each couple of passengers as they filed aboard. This angel was named Meyer. He sat on the deck of the Ark, right at the head of the gangway, and as each pair of animals appeared, Meyer gave them searching looks, then chose a name.

Take the ungainly, huge-antlered, yellow-coated deer that lives in the mountains of Mongolia, for example. When they filed aboard the Ark, Meyer felt stumped, but after a while he cried, "Altai-wapiti!"

The other angels, who did not like Meyer, were watching him like whatever they called a hawk before that name was allocated. And when Meyer touched the shoulder of the huge-antlered, yellow-coated deer with his sword, saying "I dub thee Altai-wapiti!!," a snippity chorus of cherubs protested: "But Meyer, why are you calling those yellowish-coated, branch-antlered things Altai-wapiti?"

Meyer answered, "Because they *look* like Altai-wapiti, that's why."

According to legend, Noah was so impressed by this that he doubled Meyer's salary on the spot. I do not believe this.

P.S. Meyer named other deer "Hello" and "Good-bye," from which comes our custom of saying "Hello (or Good-bye), dear."

"What does a Chinese typewriter look like?"

A printer's pipe dream. A Chinese typewriter has almost 2580 "keys"—plus blank spaces into which slugs of the less common letters can be fitted. These not-common characters are kept in a reserve block of 3430. So a Chinese letter typed on a Chinese typewriter is drawn from a bank of 6010 letters.

"In one of your books you say that you clip newpapers and magazines all the time for your files. I would like to know—what is your favoritemost clipping?"

This one, from a small-town paper in Iowa:

> The baseball game between the Rockets and the Huskers was held in Mr. Simpson's cow pasture, and ended in the third inning, with the score tied 1–1, when a runnner slid into what he thought was second base.

"Can you tell me why did the Victorians give a lock of hair to someone dear to them?"

For goo and coo. But the custom began, in ancient times, because it was thought that one's "vital spirit" was secreted in the hair. If you could get hold of a person's hair, you could (presumably) put the whammy on him. (Cf. Samson and the Philistines.)

To show the depth of their love, people began giving locks of their hair to each other. It was like saying, "I put my life in your hands." That's considerably more romantic than "I put my hair in your mouth."

"Who holds the world's record for hitting consecutive foul balls?"

I do. On June 30, 1968, I hit 247 consecutive foul balls in a now-famous match between the Canarsie Cowards and the Valparaiso Vultures. The umpire, Barney ("Butch") Raskolnikov, later told the press, and I quote: "This is the most amazing feat of cunning or ineptitude anyone has seen since the palmiest days of 'Babe' Herman."

Mr. Herman, as any Brooklyn Dodgers acolyte remembers, used to try to catch fly balls on his head, had a tendency to place lighted cigars in his pockets, and once negated his own home run by zooming around the bases, jaw clenched and eyes glazed, with such determination that he passed two of his goggle-eyed teammates who happened to be on the bases ahead of him. This unorthodox maneuver invalidated three runs, robbed two teammates of their powers of speech and enraged a thousand Flatbush fans, who remained delirious for weeks.

To return to the game in which I made my mark: It did not break up for three nights, since it takes quite a long time to hit 247 foul balls. My feat made all the Vultures' relief pitchers very cross. Nothing upsets southpaws so much as having a stubborn man at bat— especially one with foul breadth.

"Do you know of a good book explaining collapsed arches?"

Occasionally.

"Mealy bugs, aphids and other harmful pests are in our garden. What is a good book that can tell me how to get rid of these pests?"

"Let Us Spray," by Rachel Carson.

"My husband and I often read you, and he gets very angry with me because I do not agree with him. Whom do you think is right?"

If he likes my work, him is right. If he doesn't, youm is. Divorce him.

Liking the same writer is much more important to a marriage than any other single factor. I don't care what your marriage counselor told you about extended foreplay in sex.

"Who was the first man in history to cross the United States on roller skates? It is my ambition to do something like that."

He was crazy. So are you.

"Does any animal sleep with its eyes open?"

The Elephant Shrew, which looks like a baby kangaroo, never closes its eyes. Apparently.

This shrew sleeps with its eyes wide open not because it is shrewd, or even smart, but because that's the type of shrew that outsurvived less suspicious ancestors.

"Can you explain what is a Spoonerism?"

A type of metathesis. (Come back! Listen!) "Metathesis" only means a verbal boo-boo created by the mistaken transposition of the opening sounds of successive words: "The Lord is a shoving leopard" for "The Lord is a loving shepherd," or the mistaken reversal of words in familiar phrases: "Work is the curse of the drinking class."

The Power of Positive Nonsense

The term "spoonerism" honors (if that's the right word) the excitable Reverend W. A. Spooner (1844–1930), an absent-minded slip-of-the-tongue genius who was Warden of New College, Oxford. Among Spooner's most celebrated fluffs are these, which glow in my memory:

"It is kisstomary to cuss the bride."

"Victoria, our queer old dean."

"You all know what it is to have a half-warmed fish burning within you" (for "a half-formed wish").

"Remember our two great romantic poets, Sheets and Kelley."

My favorite is the triple-decker: "Young man, you have hissed my mystery lecture, virtually tasted this whole worm, and someone saw you fight a liar on High Street!"

Had I had any may in the satter, Spooner would have been rewarded sith a weat in the Louse of Hords.

Lest you think Spoonerisms a quaint relic of Victorian times, may I remind you of the refulgent boo-boos on radio and television? My Golden Book of Boners gives four stars to the following:

"Now to our announcer in the stadium for the ballcast of the broad game."

"And now—stay stewed for the nudes!"

"For Christmas, why not give your wife a Gorgeous Gruen?"*

I could raise your hair with transpositions of letters that led to most vulgar gaffes, but my respect for finicky readers impels me to suggest that you figure out for your-

---

* Repeat, increasing tempo, and lightning will strike you.

self how announcers came croppers with risky names which, mispronounced, became risqué howlers:

Friar Tuck

World Cup Soccer

Tucker Frederickson

"How do the honky-tonk pianos in Western movies produce that tinny 'plink–prrring–prrrang' which so perfectly suits the setting?"

The metallic tintinnabulations in cowboy flicks always made me think there was a crazed cat trapped inside the piano box, frantically plucking the wires with its claws. I have just learned that the "plunk-plink-prrrrang"-ing is achieved simply by stripping off the felt pads of the hammers that strike the piano's wires. This magnifies the wires' percussive reverberations and gave civilization the maniacal sound which has come to symbolize the "Aw shucks, ma'am" world of John Wayne, Wyatt Earp, professional gunmen and painted floozies who help the virtuous hero slay the forces of Evil anywhere west of Wichita. One of the full-bosomed gals usually gets mixed up in the final shoot-out and is sure to be hit by the vile villain's bullet—thus saving the life of the valiant hero, who has never even *kissed* her. The splendid Code of the West maintained that a lady's nobility surpassed her wanton trade.

When a golden-hearted harlot died, the upright piano never made a low-down sound.

"How long is a giraffe's tongue?"

About eighteen inches—but why in the world are you interested in *that?*

"Who invented the windshield wiper?"

I think I did.

"Why are they called 'digital' computers?"

Because they make it possible for people to count without using their fingers. As you know, people have been
counting on their digits for centuries. Bookkeepers used
to count their fingers to the bone, and children who bit
their nails found it hard to do fractions. That is why
educators ever since Maria Montessori had been begging
mathematicians to develop an automatic counting device.

The first computer was invented by Antoine Paskudnyak, the famous Esthonian bugler, whose fingers had
given out after twenty-six years of playing the Esthonian
national anthem. Paskudnyak's counting machine cleverly used pinballs instead of batteries. Where it failed
was in handling decimal points, since it is an old Esthonian custom never to point at a decimal. Paskudnyak
ended up in a mental institution.

The *great* computer breakthrough came in our own
country (and we can all be mighty proud of that,
folks) in 1946, when Shlomo Omo, a mathematical
wizard in one of our Think-thanks, discovered that by
using simple "on–off" electric switches he could create
an entirely new numerical vocabulary. Omo's sapience
lay in treating "on" as 1, and "off" as o. By arranging
and extending these two digits, any number could be
translated into the new computer language! Thus:

$$00 = 0$$
$$01 = 1$$

$$11 = 2$$
$$10 = 3$$
$$101 = 4$$
$$111 = 5$$

and so on. A number like 7436 (the average tonnage of cod trawlers in Iceland) involved a great many figures (10111001010100001001111111111010100001, to be exact). Omo, who believed in shlo motion, had a heart attack.

His work was carried on by his wife Selma, and in no time at all her application of Shlomo's dazzling digitry brought the marvelous new world of electronic computers into being. They have been there ever since.

"How far can birds fly?"

Very. Barn swallows from Alaska travel 9000 miles (!), all the way down to Patagonia.

Is this a fantastic distance, compared to other feathered flights? It is not. Storks from Copenhagen regularly cross the Mediterranean and the entire continent of Africa to get to the southeast part thereof: 8000 miles.

Whether the children of Capetown think those Danish storks fly in with diapers in their beaks, carrying babies who will create severe sibling rivalry, has not yet been studied by social scientists. That shows you how far behind us South Africa is in critical research.

"I do not have many friends and sure would like to. Can you help me? What can a person do to be popular?"

It is very easy to be popular. Just ask people for advice.

Don't pay attention to the answers. Just ask for advice. You will be amazed by how swiftly the word gets around that you are a "beautiful human being," warmhearted, open-minded and *exceptionally* sound of judgment.

"What's the craziest contest you ever heard of?"

The one in 1965, when some far-out Englishmen started a competition in which the participants had to demolish upright pianos and pass the wreckage through a ten-inch ring. They could use any tools, but sledgehammers were limited to seven pounds.

It took a team of three students from the Medway College of Art only three minutes eleven seconds to pulverize their piano.

"Is it true that a pig always sleeps on its right side?"

Certainly. Pigs always sleep on their right side because, I think, they hate to be wrong.

"When was the name 'America' first used?"

Forty-seven years after Columbus discovered the New World. "America" was never used by Columbus. Martin Waldseemüller, cosmographer, was the first to use the appellation—for two continents.

"Where do those Catholics who still do not eat meat once a week not eat meat on Wednesdays?"

In Saudi Arabia. There, both Catholics and Protestants observe Friday, not Sunday, as the Sabbath. Why? Because Muslims celebrate their Sabbath on Fridays. The oil companies where Catholics and Protestants work decided to close on Fridays, instead of Sundays, to keep everything on an even keel even in the desert of Saudi Arabia.

"How did Antwerp get its name?"

Antwerp means "the place of hand throwing." That's because, some six hundred years ago, the inhabitants of the place used to cut the right hand off a thief and throw it into the Scheldt River. Maybe they were trying to impress him with the maxim "Thou scheldt not steal."

"Why do we call a big shot a 'big cheese'?"

Because *chiz* is the Persian/Urdu word for "thing."
"Eh? *What?*" you blink. "How does a Persian/Urdu word get into English?"
Easily. The phrase crept into English via the amused British sahibs of India and was elaborated upon in the vernacular back home to mean anything important or consequential.

"Some joker told me that the people in the rear of a studio audience at a broadcast actually hear the program later than someone listening on a radio 400 miles away. What would you say to a guy like that?"

I would say, "Thank you." The joker was telling the truth.
Sound waves, which you hear in the studio, travel much more slowly than radio waves, which you hear from the loudspeaker in your set.

The velocity of sound is not constant, but varies according to temperature and the media through which it passes. In the air (as opposed to solids, liquids or gas), sound travels at 1130 feet per second—at 20 degrees centigrade. But radio waves radiate at a little less than the speed of light—which is a stupendous 186,000 miles per second.

No wonder we hear a radio broadcast 500 (to say nothing of 400) miles away faster than the people 200 feet away in the studio, which is usually too cold for comfort.

"What's your favorite story about filling out application cards?"

The one involving the sweet young thing who applied for her first job by filling out the form this way:

> *Date of birth:* Feb. 7, 1959
> *Weight:* 6 pounds, 10 ounces
> *Height:* 20 inches
> *Color of hair:* None

"I am always mixed up about when to use 'that' or 'who' and when to use 'which.' Can you explain?"

No, I cannot explain why you always get mixed up about when to use "that" or "who" and when to use "which."

But I can clear up the confusion, so widespread and vexatious, about when to use each of these fine, patriotic adjectives:

1. Use "that" when referring to articles made of cork or feathers.

2. Never say "*Who?*" when discussing U.N. delegates from underdeveloped countries. They resent being hard to identify.
3. Use "which" for shredded wheat.
4. Never use "that" when discussing "which," but don't hesitate to use "which" when discussing "that."
5. Always use "who" when referring to owls. Even better is the use of "who-who."
6. The only times to use "that which" is when:

   a. you are discussing the historic trials in Salem, Mass.;
   b. you are on the witness stand and have been asked to point to the woman in the courtroom who has done most to give you shingles. If the judge rules that you are using "which" as a pejorative pun for "witch" (which you are) and asks you to rephrase your answer, reply, "Who?"

      He will answer, "You."

      That's when you smile: "You who?"

      And that's when you get the heave-ho (not "hoo") for contempt of court.

"Can you tell me anything about Formosus, Landus and Eulalius?"

Only by looking up the names, with considerable grumbling. I *thought* there would be a yummy connection between the three names, but all I can find is that they were popes. Formosus was pope from 891 to 896, when he died. Landus was pope from 913 to 914. Eulalius, whose name suggests the famous Hawaiian musical instrument, was an antipope, from 418 to 419.

I'll bet you thought you'd stump me.

"What's the largest fresh-water fish in the world? I don't mean whales."

The sword-billed sturgeon (*Psephorus gladius*), which frequents the larger rivers of China. One of these giants weighed 1600 pounds (!) when caught in the Yellow River, back in 1927. Some of these sturgeons grow up to twenty feet long.

I don't mean whales, either.

"I hear that some bricks float. Is that true?"

Sure. They're made of very light clay. What kind of clay is that light? Clay of volcanic origin. (Oh, stop sulking.)

"Is it true that in Borneo pregnant women try never to sleep during a rain?"

That's what I hear. Where did you hear it, Buster?

"Can a citrus tree grow lemons and oranges at the same time?"

Shucks, there's a citrus tree that bears oranges, lemons, limes, grapefruit and kumquats at the same time. What wonders hath Burbank wrought....

"Who are the world's most passionate movie fans?"

I would have guessed the Romans. Or the Japanese! That's what's wrong with guessing.

More people go to the movies in Macao than anywhere else. Macauans have *averaged* 28.4 movies per
person per year, and that—says the *Guinness Book of
Records*—is the world's record.

I did not know cinematophilia could reach such depths.

"How powerful is nuclear force?"

Well, it can pull and hold particles together until they
reach a density of one billion tons per cubic inch. You
read that right: one billion *tons* per cubic inch.

The density of a collapsed star is so incredibly enormous that the best way to describe it is to say that a
matchbox full of the stuff would weigh 40,000 pounds.
Try to find a match for that.

"My wife is a wiz at Brain-teasers and she gave me one I can't figure out and it is driving me nuts and she needles me about being so dumb so can you give me the answer? (Send it to the above address, my office, so I can spring the answer on her at home and knock her for a loop!) Here is the brain-teaser she keeps needling me about:

"Horace is 2 years younger than his sister, Mame, and is losing his teeth. Mame is 4 years older than the cheerleader of their school in Great Neck. The janitor, who is always whistling, night and day, is 72.

The total age of these four people is 183. What's the principle's name?

I am surprised you find this brain-teaser difficult. The
clues are so obvious that the answer is a cinch:

1. "Night and Day" was written by Cole Porter,
which is a perfect name for a janitor.

2. The difference between "principle" and "principal" is seven.

3. If Horace is losing his teeth while two years younger than his sister, put the blame on Mame.

4. If the janitor is seventy-two, he should quit, collect social security, and learn to yodel. Whistling when you're over seventy can get you into a lot of trouble these days.

5. So . . . the principal's name is not Apparent. It is Theodore Feldman, which is the most popular name for high school principals in Great Neck.

P.S. If I had a wife like yours, I would fill my back yard with quicksand.

"Can you recommend a psychiatrist who will come to my house and treat my wife, who is forty-seven and so scared of snakes she never leaves the house?"

You don't need a psychiatrist. Buy a mongoose.

"Am madly in love with a wonderful girl who is madly in love with me and though we are nineteen years old, still are madly in love. Our parents are against it. Should we get married?"

No. Being madly in love is a good reason for not getting married. Love is a dangerous illness, marked by high fevers, bad English and a paralysis of judgment. Important decisions should never be made in this state. Marriage should only be undertaken in cold blood, and on a full stomach.

I suggest you stay madly in love until you are both forty-three.

Fan Mail

"What is the quickest way how someone gets to be a 'pro' writer?"

The quickest way how someone gets to be a "pro" writer is by composing petitions in support of causes, like DISARM TODAY! or GET LOST! That will put you in the *pro* ranks at once.

If you want to be a "con" writer, on the other hand, compose patriotic petitions *against* things, like BOYCOTT EGYPTIAN MEZUZAHS! or STAMP OUT JUNGLE FEVER!

"Can you explain how that triumph of electronics, the Palm-Sized Calculator, actually works?"

Gladly. The Palm-Sized Calculator is not only a triumph of electronics; it is also an absolute wizard at showing you how slow, sloppy, unreliable or stupid you were before. Let me illustrate:

Suppose you want to add 29 to 92. Just punch the 2 button, then the 9, then the "+" button, then punch 9, then 2, then the "=" key. The answer will instantly appear as "o"—because you forgot to throw the "ON–OFF" switch to "ON." Whenever you don't do that, the genie who works inside the magical mechanism is at his office and not in yours.

Let's begin over. First, throw the switch to "ON." Don't *touch* the switch; snap it. Don't just depress the switch either, because that will depress you—since the "ON" position, out of all the keys/buttons before you, is the only one that will work only if it is switched, and the only one which doesn't register the slightest touch, breath or breeze, which all the others do. In fact, all the others respond to pressures you are not even aware of, such as your yawning. If you cough, God forbid, everything on the keyboard doubles.

Another important tip: It is best to be naked, or wear very short sleeves, while using a calculator. The merest brush of your cuff can set off a chain reaction; the touch of a sleeve button may rip across a whole row of numbers and multiply everything by 456. If you move full sleeve half an inch, the results are even more unnerving. Numbers will pop up on the blue-green display panel (say 680) and then vanish; that's because you accidentally hit the "C" key, which stands for "Correct." In electronic-calculator language, "correct" doesn't mean "right"—it means "wipe off" the last number touched.

Let's start over. Flip the "ON–OFF" switch to "ON." At once, your friendly little calculator will light up with neon pleasure. (It gets pretty lonely for the gnome down there in the dark with no one to talk to except cold numbers huddled together like bats in a cave.) When a calculator is turned to "ON" it gets so happy it turns a luminous bluish-green.

Very well. Remember: we want to add 29 and 92. So, with "ON" glowing, press the 2 button, then the 9, then 9, then 2. To get the total, touch the "=" button and the answer will appear in a flash:

2992

That is wrong, because 29 plus 92 equals 121, not 2992. The reason for the 2992 is simple: you forgot to press the "+" button after you pressed 29 and before you pressed 92. You must be very careful to do that, because the "+" button is neurotically sensitive and sulks if you don't touch it fondly when its turn has come. (This, incidentally, is not true of the "—" button, which is always grateful to be caressed. That is because Minus signs are universally despised and are nowhere as pushy as Plus signs, which is why Plus gets most of the business.)

Now, suppose you want to multiply. That is as easy as pie—unless you press the "π" button, which means 3.12146 and always comes in second in high school hatred polls; ratios are first.

Let's see how to multiply 32 by 11. Touch the 3, then the 2, then the "×" key, then the 1, then the 1 again, then the "=." The answer will be either 32100000 (because you accidentally touched the "REP" or "CHAIN CAL" button) or 0 (because your batteries conked out).

Start over. Life is not all sunshine and roses. Press 3, then 2, then "×," then 1, then 1 again, then "=." Good. Now if the answer is "0" it shows you accidentally touched the "AC" button, which means "ALL CLEAR"— *i.e.,* all the numbers are wiped off the scoreboard. It is astonishing how agile that "AC" button is. I know a mathematician who was working out a tough problem on calculus, using the best electronic calculator. At the crucial point in his labors, he got the hiccups. The machine promptly reported the annual consumption of rum in the Virgin Islands.

This brings me to the "." button. That is the decimal point and must be touched when you are working with dollars and cents. Even the most inept ignoramus in arithmetic will swiftly learn that the "." button was shrewdly put there to drive him nuts. Let's see how this ingenious button works. Suppose you want to add $12.10 to $4.83. You can't press the "$" key, because the manufacturers do not put a "$" key on the keyboard. So, to add the numbers above, simply press 1, 2, . , 1, 0. Now press the "+" button. Then press 4, 8, 3. Okay. Now touch that heart-warming, ever-ready, thank-God-it's-over-button, the "=." The answer will flash in ecstasy on the colorful display panel. It may be $12,104.83, which is wrong, or "0," or "000," but there it is, and for an obvious reason. I wish I knew what it is.

"Who invented the ball-point quill?"

I did.

"In your opinion who was the greatest shortstop of all times?"

In my opinion, I was the greatest shortstop of all time. The only shortstop who was shorter was Polonius ("Pee-Wee") Pincus, who played for the New Haven Nudnicks. "Pee-Wee" was so short that even with cleats on his Adler lift shoes he could walk under the tables down at Mory's.

"Why do the inhabitants of Iowa get cancer so much more often than the natives of Burundi?"

Because they live so much longer. Cancer rates increase with age. The longer you live, the more chance you have of dying—from all sorts of things. More Bostonians that Burundians need pacemakers, wear dentures or become senile.

"Is it true that more people who own Rolls-Royces suffer from arthritis than do people who own jalopies?"

Absolutely. You have to be rich to own a Rolls. The chances of your being rich (or becoming rich) increase with age. So do your chances of getting arthritis.

"Do you know of a cure for rheumatism?"

No, but I know a dozen loony cures in which people have invested faith. The following are authentic—facts, not cures:

Having a woman who bore a child feet first (I mean the child's feet) attend to the rheumatism sufferer.

Wearing silver rings made from the hinges of coffins.

Rubbing red peppers under the toenails.

Carrying a stolen potato.

Burying the afflicted one (up to the neck only) in a churchyard. The longer he or she stays there, the more potent the therapy. (I suppose they have a rheum of their own.)

"How fast can bees move their wings?"

Honeybees move their wings up and down around 200 times a second, giving the bees a velocity of five to ten m.p.h.

Why didn't you ask me about their flying range, which is phenomenal? Bees fly as far as sixty miles a day when collecting food. Thank you.

"I hear that houses in Tokyo are numbered in a peculiar way. Is that true?"

It certainly is. Houses in Tokyo are numbered according to the order in which the building permits were issued. Their numbers bear no resemblance whatsoever to the location of the house, nor to the numbers to the left and right of it.

Let me clarify this mare's nest. Suppose the houses in, say, Alhambra (Cal.) were numbered Nipponese style: 807 Fremont Street might be next to 1641 on one side, 952 on the other and 28 across the way.

In the building-permits files at Alhambra's City Hall, a typical page would read:

> #3841—6/7/48—Abe Cumquat
> #3842—6/8/48—Nelly Le Brun
> #3843—6/9/48—Howard Snattle

Now Mr. Cumquat might put up a shack on Marengo Street numbered 3841, Madam Le Brun might build a bordello on Stoneman Avenue numbered 3842, and Mr. Snattle might erect a mansion on South Atlantic Road numbered 3843.

I cannot blame you for wondering how in the world anyone in Tokyo manages to get to the right address. I'll tell you how. Your host writes or telephones extremely detailed instructions. When I was invited to visit a learned professor in Tokyo, for instance, I followed his travel orders to a T:

> Go to Sukyaki Bank, just beyond Tetsumaka shrine. Pass bank until you see rock nursery. Turn left. Pass peach trees to pagoda on left. Proceed to Takishamaya Skating Rink. Stop. Opposed to rink is Nagiku Herb Emporium. Tell your driver to ask proprietor to provide directions to Professor Michio-san.

So equipped, I easily met disaster. Since a Japanese would sooner disembowel himself than insult you by saying "I don't know," we were misdirected with counterfeit confidence by four successive residents of the neighborhood.

My driver finally had to phone my host and tell him where we were marooned. The professor sent a kimonoed servant to clop-clop to us on her *getas* to show us the way home. Her repeated bowing gave and told me vertigo.

"What is your favorite bird?"

The Pileated Tinamou, found in picturesque Panama. It sings every three hours—*every* three hours, day and night. (Panama's national anthem must be "Of Three I Sing.")

"Who were the Locofocos?"

Don't be disgusting. They were merely a minor American political party. Other fanciful names given to, or taken by, our offbeat political groups: Coolies, Barnburners, Hunkies, Bucktails, Mugwumps—who were somewhat saner than Locofocos.

Please don't ask me to identify them. Any good book on American history has an index.

"Why is 'honeymoon' used for the first rapturous days of marriage?"

Because wedded amour was oft compared to the full moon—which, alas, swiftly wanes.

"I don't suppose you know how the Christmas custom of hanging empty stockings before the fireplace began?"

If that's what you suppose, why did you write me?

It is said that St. Nicolas heard about three sisters who were so penniless that they could scarcely go on living, so St. Nick appeared over their hut, which had no chimney but merely a hole in the roof, and tossed three gold pieces through the smoke. The gold pieces landed not on the hearth but in the stockings which the three little poor girls had hung up to dry.

Since then, children have been hanging their stockings at, on or near the fireplace.

"Who is your favorite humorist?"

My favorite humorist is Hamish Cooze, a kneecap designer who never met the great Sam Goldwyn, yet tossed off these imperishable apothegms:

> "If your father was alive, he'd turn over in his grave."
>
> "*No* one ever goes to that restaurant—it's too crowded!"
>
> "I'd give my right arm to have you as my right hand."
>
> "It's a lousy movie; don't fail to miss it if you can."
>
> "My wife has such beautiful hands I'm going to have a sculptor make a bust of them."

If you can top these, let me know.

"Can you tell me the exact difference between a neurotic and a psychotic—or should I ask a psychiatrist?"

If you say "Hello" to a psychiatrist he will charge you

fifty bucks. You've come to the right man: I only charge ten. Here is the answer to your question:

A *psychotic* is an out-and-out loon. He may think that his wife is stealing his dreams, his boss is planning to garotte him with noodles, or that two plus two equals eight.

A *neurotic,* on the other hand, is an in-and-out sufferer, afflicted by things like anxiety, underarm humidity or the feeling that Las Vegas should be flooded with garotte him with noodles, or that two plus two equals four—but he just can't *stand* it.

"Why do children think spitting is a way to increase their strength (as in spitting on your palms before tackling a job), or a way to insure good luck, or to ward off demons?"

Not only children, by a long shot, attach magic to expectoration. That's why Irishmen spit into their palms before fighting and why lumberjacks do likewise before wielding an axe.

Down the centuries, and in any number of cultures, saliva has been considered part of one's soul—and to spit was/is to make an offering to whatever gods the credulous believe in. Examples:

In many parts of the Middle East, the Balkans, Russia and India, spitting on the closed eyes of a blind person is supposed to restore sight.

In South Africa, the Baronga spit whenever they see a shooting star.

In Guatemala, whenever an Indian passes a cairn (at a road crossing or on a cliff top) he spits on grass which he lays on the topmost flat stone.

In Scotland, learned or wise men were once paid a
fee to spit on sick animals or on cows whose teats
had dried up.

In Madagascar, spitting at the door from inside a
sick relative's room or house is supposed to make the
demons inside the sick one scoot away. The sick, in
Madagascar, also spit like crazy to accelerate the farewell of their undesired *dybbuks*, which is not a Mada-
gascarian word.

In many European countries, the Catholic priests at a
christening used to touch the baby on the nostrils and
behind the ears with a little spittle—then applied holy
water to the forehead.

I will be happy to swear before a notary that all the
above *mishegoss* has been culled from reliable, sober
sources.

"Where does the expression 'Popeye' come from?"

Popeye or Popeyes, which is more accurate, is/are a
symptom of hyperthyroidism. Goiter, which is an en-
largement of the thyroid gland, is another sign. The disease leads to weight loss and jitters because it shoots the
basal metabolism (burning up of carbons, fats, and proteins) way up. The popeyed part, technically known as
exophthalmos, comes from the pressure of the greatly
enlarged thyroid gland.

Cheer up. The disease is curable—by either iodine
(radioactive) therapy or frank, blunt surgery.

And popeyes are not limited to sailors—or spinach.

Fan Mail

"Can you tell me how I can find a wife who will not yak, yak, yak, yak at me all the time?"

No, no, no, no.

"Do you believe there is a life after death, or do we just die and nothing happens after?"

Yes.

"Which politicians do you most (and least) admire?"

The politician I most admire is the English bucko who proclaimed, "I promise you that if I am elected, I will be neither partial nor impartial."

The politician I most despise is the flimflammer who told the voters in Florida, in a campaign against Senator Claude Pepper: "Did you know that my opponent once *matriculated* at college? That he openly practices *monogamy?* That his sister works in New York as a well-known *thespian!*"

Poor Pepper was clobbered at the polls.

"Who is the world champ Pole-Vaulter?"

I am.

"My parents gave our little Tommy a full-grown Shetland pony for his birthday. He (the pony) often raises his ears, kicks his hind legs, brays like hell and won't budge an inch! What can we do about this? Tommy goes into a state of shock whenever he fails to mount the pony."

Are you sure you have a pony? From the way the beast behaves, it would not surprise me if your parents did not give your little boy a full-grown pony but a young mule. I have heard of Shetland ponies praying, but never braying.

I suggest you take pictures of the creature and send them (or it) to your state Department of Animal Husbandry. Government agencies are very skillful in shettling arguments about ponies.

"In what play did Brutus say 'I have come to bury Caesar, not to praise him'?"

In Shakespeare's *Death of a Salesman.*

"My brother-in-law, Walter, is such a big worrier he is a pain in the ass. I'm the type who never lets anything bug me. I can truthfully say, I am happy all the time."

Anyone who is happy all the time is nuts.

I don't know Walter, who may have a Krankheit from watching television; but if I were you, I'd count my marbles twice a day.

"My son loves his job in a garage (fixing cars) and does not want to go to college! His Dad and I keep after him all the time, but he says he isn't the college type! What should we do?"

Apologize. We need good mechanics more than lousy students.

"My son who is very bowlegged and he is going with a pidgeon-Toed girl. What kind of children do you think they will have?"

Confused.

"Who is your favorite not-real demon or spook?"

Tanchelin, who supposedly lived in Hungary/Romania in the twelfth century. This maleficent creep possessed such satanic powers that fearful husbands begged him to sleep with their wives. I think Tanchelin was less of a ghoul than a con man. What a pity he never wrote his memoirs.

My next favorite demon was "the Grand Chancellor of Hell," the evil spirit Adrammlech. The Assyrians worshipped Adrammlech. This is not surprising if you remember that that goblin could assume the shape of either a peacock or a mule, which runs a praiseworthy gamut of disguises.

Close on Adrammlech's heels in my affections is the redoubtable Amduscias, "Grand Duke of Hell," who was shaped like a unicorn. He gave vocal recitals at no charge to his gulls. He did not even charge the boys.

"My biology teacher told us that grasshoppers make their buzzing sounds by rubbing their back legs together. Is this true?"

This is one of the most ridiculous prejudices law-abiding grasshoppers have to put up with. Grasshoppers make those buzzing noises not by rubbing their back legs together but by blowing on tiny kazoos which they conceal under their wings. The male makes the "Zzz" sound and the female makes the "Bzz" sound.

Sometimes a grasshopper will produce both a "Zzz" and a "Bzz" sound simultaneously, like this: "ZzzBzzZzz." That means you are listening to a grasshopper who is either confused or asleep.

"In English novels they are always giving someone's weight not in pounds but in 'stones.' How can I find out how many pounds are in a stone?"

Weigh the stone, dummy.

"Which one man or woman do you think has done the most for the human race?"

Whitcomb L. Judson. He invented the zipper.

"Do big, strange, fancy words help a writer's style?"

Hallucal energy, kyphosis, or even gongeozling will avail you naught. For each word is worthy of isonomy.

Don't think I shall clatterclaw you as a jobbernowl for verbal labefaction or eisegesis. Your conatus in eutaxy should justify jactitation, my gossoon, even if it be fugacious.

Apolaustic writers find thrawn pleasure in such orgulous, epexegetic exercises, but I, from my coign, respond with narial disdain, thou slubberdegullion.

This monstrous romp should cure you of reverence for the obscure. The display of erudition is not laudable.

Translated into the comprehensible, the dreadful diction above means:

The energy of your big toe, a curvature of the spine, or even intensive staring will not help you. Each word is worthy of equal rights.

Don't think I'll abuse you as having a stupid

head or verbal weakening, or for presenting your own thoughts as if they were another's. Your effort at pleasing arrangement should justify boasting, my boy, even if it be fleeting.

Self-indulgent writers find perverse pleasure in such haughty, explanatory exercises, but I, from my point of observation, respond with nasal disdain, you base wretch.

That should answer your question.

"I am a High School Junior interested in Birds, specially the Toucan which is my favorate, being so colorfull, so please send full information for the term paper I have to write."

You should stop studying Birds and switch to Spelling.

Toucans, which are as colorful as they are colorfull, are oviparous vertebrates. This does not mean they hide porous eggs in their vertebra.

Toucans are very popular with other birds in the feathered family of *Aves*, because they try harder. They also enjoy beer in bottles.

Toucans mate earlier than most birds because according to their religion toucan live cheaper than one.

"Who invented Morse code?"

· — – — ·· – · — — ·· ··· ··· ·

"Where do you get your ideas for your books?"

That's a *dan*dy question.

" . . . so I enclose a sample of my writing. Do you think I should go in for Journalism with a chance to break into the big time, or would I be better off going into Dentistery or taking up some other line like my folks keep adviseing me to?"

Obviously.

"I began writing when I was 16 but since I married and had 3 children, I have just left my writeing go. I would like to get back and make my name in the writeing field. Do you have any good sudgestions?"

I have two good suggestions: (1) Have three more children, the sooner the better. (2) Don't help your children with their homework.

"Who invented four-wheel brakes?"

I did.

"We had a big argument in our English class about when you knock on a door and the occupant calls, 'Who's there?' Do you answer, 'It's I' or 'It's me'?"

What grade are you in? I answer, "It's Merwyn P. Schlumpenbock of Yum Yum, Tennessee." My name is not Merwyn P. Schlumpenbock, but there certainly is a town called Yum Yum in Tennessee. Its zip code is 38390.

" . . . why does our country honor politicians or football heroes instead of the true benefactors of mankind— like the genius who discovered penicillin?"

Thank you.

"What do you think are the basic things we ought to know about human behavior?"

1. *Everyone* had "an unhappy childhood."

2. No two children are ever born into the same family. (The first child has no siblings, the second has one, the third has two.... The parents of a second child are different from what they were with their first.)

3. No one ever does anything for only one reason.

4. Most people never mature; they just grow taller.

5. Everyone, in some small, sacred sanctuary of the self, is nuts.

6. Imagination, not conscience, makes cowards of us all.

7. It is impossible to name anything, however wonderful, which won't depress some people. It is impossible to name anything, however horrible, which won't elate other people.

8. Some people will do anything for money; more will do anything for nothing. Kicks (and delusions) are more influential than lucre.

9. No tyranny is more subtle, infuriating and invincible than the tyranny of neurotics. Their suffering is a weapon, no less than a symptom.

10. Beware of people without a sense of humor. Its absence shows a lack of proportion, uneasy self-respect, and a fear of those secure enough to be tolerant of vices other than their own.

"Do you believe that man is the missing link?"

Why not? I believe, with Konrad Lorenz, that

man is the missing link—between apes and human beings. Well, as I confessed at the beginning of this tone poem, each year's end gives me the exhilaration of truthfully replying to my readers—in my fantasies. This helps restore my self-esteem, which has been grumbling and growling around the house for a year, muttering, "Coward! Coward!" My imaginary answers, so swift in scorn, so flashing in riposte, reward me for the odious politeness I have so nobly observed lo! twelve moody, anguished months.

And now, my valedictory: To all like me who flinch from candor; who too gently desist from hurting the feelings of morons; who shed sweetness and light upon undeserving pests and *paskudnyaks;* who patiently bear bores, brats and buttonholers; who placate tummlers, shmos, shleppers and shlemiels; who bite their tongues before answering needlers, wheedlers, nerds and wisenheimers; who make pious allowances for creeps and nudnicks; who suffer the stings and harrows of letters from nitwits too lazy to look up the answers themselves, or too cheap to buy an almanac or seed catalogue that would slake their slack-jawed curiosity; to all like me who take refuge behind the ignoble palisades of etiquette: Happy New Year.

(*Lord*, I feel better.)

5.
SEEING
IS
DECEIVING

"How saintly people look
when seasick."

—*Samuel Butler*

I was curled up with a good cook the other night (my wife happens to be a *very* good cook), when I ran across a passage that made me gasp in a manner that can only be described as—oh, midway between disbelief and rapture.

My wife, I am happy to say, did not ask, "Why are you gasping in a manner that can only be described as—oh, midway between disbelief and rapture?"

"I have just run across a gorgeous, unbelievable fact," I chortled. "One-fourth of all the marriages in our country take place between a boy and a girl *who live or lived within five blocks of each other!*"

"That's nice," said my wife.

"And in *half* of all the marriages in the United States, the bride and groom lived within twenty blocks of each other!"

"Do tell," she yawned.

"*These*," I said sternly, "are *facts!*"

"I don't believe them."

"You don't '*believe*' them?" I gasped. "What do you mean you don't '*believe*' them? They are official figures, analyzed by reputable scholars!"

"Like who?"

"I happen to be quoting from *The Principles of Sociology*," I said, "by Professors Freedman, Hawley, Landecker, Lenski and Miner!"

"Oh, soci*olog*ists," sighed Mrs. Cynic, with the sort of sigh she would employ if saying, "Oh, those poor shnooks who have to earn a living by stuffing little onions into pitted olives."

"Some of our best friends are sociologists!" I declaimed.

"That's not their fault."

"Very funny. The trouble with you is that you have no respect for science."

"The trouble with you," she smiled with infuriating kindliness, "is that you are a patsy for facts."

I slapped the covers of my book together so hard that Lenski fell into Landecker's lap. "And I used to wonder why people say I made a morganatic marriage!" I hurled my head upon my pillow in a way that would have left no doubt in the mind of a sensitive woman that she had gone too far. My wife kissed my cheek unfairly, chuckling, "Good night, fact freak."

What can you do with a woman like that?

It's certainly true that I *am* kind of nutsy about facts. I collect and cherish and rub my hands greedily over them. Oh, I don't mean I go around buying up rare specimens at auction. And I certainly don't shower affection on every silly filly of a fact that comes down the pike—you know, the kind newspapers use as space-fillers, of which a rousing example is: "The Frazila of Zanzibar is a unit of weight: 35 pounds."

I *hate* a fact like that. It has no pizzazz; it doesn't get, go or lead you anywhere. I don't even give a hoot about the height of Old Baldy, or the state bird of Oklahoma, which happens to be the Scissor-tailed Flycatcher.

The facts I like are twinkle-eyed and juicy, elves that tickle the ribs or electrify the mind. Take the name of the late Secretary-General of the United Nations: U Thant. Now, the "U" (pronounced *oo*, not *you*) is "Mister" in Burmese, in which "Thant" meant clean; so the late and illustrious Secretary-General of the United Nations was actually Mr. Clean! Don't tell me that isn't worth knowing.

The facts I hoard and cherish with the greatest pleasure are those which knock popular, accepted beliefs into a cocked hat. I have already given you a caboodle of such beliefs. Now let me tickle your ribs with some examples of *visible* perception and consensus.

Seeing is universally held to be decisive as evidence. "Seeing is believing." But in any number of disturbing instances seeing is deceiving—even if you are as sober as a Mormon, have 20/20 vision and long ago learned that all is not cold that shivers. I shall illustrate my thesis with some goodies that should shiver your timbers:

1. "Thar she blows!"

Like hell she does. I mean the whale does not blow water up in the high spout we have so often seen in sailors' paintings or engravings. I don't *care* how many times you've read *Moby Dick*, or seen Gregory Peck in the movie. You will just have to revise your *Weltanschauung* and accept the startling but educational fact that whales–do–not–spout–water–through–their–blow-holes.

Do I hear you protest, "But I have *seen* them spout water!"? Are you sputtering that generations of clear-eyed whalers have cried, "Thar she blows!"? when they *saw* the fountains emerge from whales' heads? I would be the last to dispute you. But what you have seen, and what generations of whaling men have been hollering about, is a different phenomenon: breathing, not spout-ing.

Pay attention: Whales have to come up for air every twenty minutes or so. They have no gills; they have lungs, which are not designed for breathing underwater. Their nostrils are on top of their heads. So the behemoth inhales—and *ex*hales—warm air and vapor. When these hit the colder outside atmosphere they condense; and it is *that* that forms the dramatic column of mist or spray.

I don't blame you or Captain Ahab for thinking that whales spout water, because it certainly looks as if they do. But all a whale is doing, while the excitable gobs in the riggings are jumping up and down, bellowing "Thar she blows!" is—exhaling. Seeing is misleading.

2. Women's Lib in Burma.

The women of Burma (ah, the women of Burma!) have for centuries walked behind their menfolk with modest and respectful mien. But after World War II, the Burmese beauties were seen (by hundreds of English and American soldiers) to be walking *ahead* of their earthly lords and masters.

This created a sensation. It led seventeen candidates

for a Ph.D. in anthropology to exclaim that at long last Democracy, with its enlightened evaluation of the role of women, had dug a toehold in the ancient Burmese culture. Some Rotarians went so far as to congratulate the men of Burma for recognizing that females are human, too, have the same feelings, hopes, dreams that men do, and are entitled to Western kindness and courtesy. It was even rumored that the League of Women Voters was considering a new branch office in Myaungmya.

Well, I hate to be a sourpuss, or even a realist, but would you like to know *why* the stalwart men of Burma permitted—nay, insisted that!—their gentle women walk in front of them? Because unexploded land mines were still buried all over the place. . . .

I will be among the first to lament the stratagem of the Burmese males as deplorable, callous and lousy. But it makes my point: Seeing is terribly deceiving.

3. The foolish ostrich.

From time immemorial (I sometimes wonder what time memorial would be like) we have all heard that the ostrich buries his head in the sand because the silly bird, who has useless wings, thinks that you can't see him when he can't see you. We smile when we ponder the ostrich's folly. And how vivid and valuable that image is when one wants to describe some piece of self-deception, some preposterous flight from reality.

There is only one thing wrong with the picture: It is untrue.

Ostriches do *not* bury their heads in the ground. They

do *not* delude themselves into thinking that you can't see them because they can't see you.

Two facts account for the ostrichian myth: First, ostriches hunt for food everywhere, and since they swallow almost anything short of iron spikes or the prose of social scientists, they (the ostriches) poke their *beaks* into any crack or cranny of the landscape. Secondly, when an ostrich tries to hide, he lays his long neck on the ground as far and as flat as he can.

Between their ways of hunting and hiding, ostriches were a set-up for that head-in-the-sand canard. End it!

4. The frantic ambulance.

How often have you seen an ambulance roaring through traffic, and heard its ear-splitting siren, and made a little prayer that the ambulance would get some poor devil to the emergency ward "in time"?

Well, Dr. R. H. Kennedy of the American College of Surgeons recently protested:

> ...speeding ambulances practically never save a life, and should be decried at every opportunity.... Often the ambulance trip is a more frightening experience than the illness or the injury.... In practically all instances, after immediate care has been rendered, the ambulance should travel carefully...without careening around corners, jamming on brakes, using the siren or going through red lights.... Too often the ambulance personnel, patients and persons outside ...are killed or injured as a result of a driver's exhibitionism.

Dr. Kennedy deserves the Voltaire Award for Candor in the Public Interest.

As for me, a veteran well-wisher to howling, careening ambulances on their rounds of mercy: When *I* go, thanks to Dr. Kennedy, I want it to be without serving as a sacrificial goat to some hopped-up driver's yearning for attention.

5. "Lemmings march down to the sea in packs of thousands and drown. Their instincts drive them to suicide."

Lemmings aren't going anywhere when they move in groups; they just get very nervous when crowded. I can find no hard evidence to support the romantic idea of a mad mass rushing to drown, in search of an ancient home in the sea.

According to Professor Charles J. Krebs of Indiana University, who has studied lemming behavior, the fables about massive lemming migrations are the misinterpretations of people who have seen lemmings during their periodic peaks of population density. "I never saw any evidence of group movements. . . ."

Dr. Krebs said this at a time when other people were clamoring that "millions of lemmings" were marching toward Hudson's Bay.

The reason for the popular myth rests on the fact that lemmings are seen in village streets and other unusual places in Scandinavia during the peak of their four-year population cycle.

As for the lemmings' purported death wish, file it under "Apocrypha." If you can't spell Apocrypha, file it under "Taradiddle."

6. Nervous elephants.

Suppose you saw a chicken sitting on an elephant's head? In a ship, plane or train, yet. What would you think?

Well, whatever conclusion you jumped to, according to Helene and Charlton Laird's *The Tree of Language*, chickens are used to keep elephants company, to calm their fears and assuage their loneliness when the pachyderms are shipped from Africa or Asia to zoos and circuses around the world.

A nervous elephant, say the Lairds, is greatly soothed by a live chicken clucking away in its vicinity. In a cage, the chickens are safest on Dumbo's head.

I feel honor-bound to report that several experts tell me they never heard of such a preposterous thing. Cluck, cluck.

7. "Boa constrictors wind themselves around victims and squeeze them to death."

They do not, even though any number of eyewitnesses will tell you that he/she saw one of the fearsome reptiles squeeze his prey into oblivion.

What the scaly scoundrel does is coil himself around a victim and when the prey breathes, exhaling air, the snake just tightens its hold. The victim again inhales (less)—and the boa tightens again. This process goes on until the victim's options run out. Then a remarkable thing happens: instantly the snake relaxes its embrace. A boa is uncannily aware of the precise moment its prey gives up the ghost.

Boas, by the bye, are not as long as legends have

duped us into believing. A boa rarely exceeds thirteen feet in length. Thirteen feet is (or are) nothing to sneeze at, of course, and I doubt whether any man or woman thrashing around in a boa's coils would want to sneeze. Nor would they gain much comfort from knowing that they are being embraced by a viper who is not thirty feet long, as many quidnuncs believe.

8. Mother Love amongst the beautiful birds.

Who has not oohed and ahed over the sight of a mama bird sitting on her eggs? And who has not marveled over the beautiful instinct of mother love in bird bosoms?

Well, I bring you mournful tidings: Birds sit on their eggs not with sentimental, loving anticipation, but for a most mundane, unromantic reason: in order to cool, relieve or soothe the inflamed "hatching spots" they develop before the nesting season. In some species, the father molts and breaks out in the rash, too, so he shares the babysitting. He does this to relieve not his mate, but his itch.

"What," you cry!

"Zounds and egad?"

"Absurd!"

"If this be true, would not *any* smooth, cool object serve the feathered matrons as well as eggs?"

The answer is Yes. That is exactly what happens if you offer a broody or brooding hen some doorknobs, or some cool, smooth stones, or ceramic Easter eggs. When their real eggs are heated, in experiments, many mothers abandon them—to search for a cooler perch on which to soothe their sensitive rashes.

Sentimental observers have seen a mother bird push out of her nest any egg not her own. True. But when Professor Johann Loeser took four eggs out of a nest of five and substituted four eggs of a different color—Mama bird promptly threw out her own (the fifth) egg.

It seems that mother birds want all their clutch to be the same color—even if it isn't the original and their own. Why the mother should prefer unfeeling symmetry to maternal schmaltz is something a Jewish boy cannot understand.

It's enough to destroy a man's faith in folklore forever.

9. Gilt by association.

In *Goldfinger*, that parody of a movie for James Bond addicts, a gorgeous sexpot is seen dead, nude, entirely gilded. She had been killed, presumably, after the application of gold paint all over her luscious body. *You* know: "We breathe through our pores—and if you seal them up, bye-bye."

Well, murder buffs, please think for a moment: Many a scoundrel was tarred and feathered in the Wild West, but did not die. Scuba divers wear airtight rubber suits, without fatal consequences. Sailors from torpedoed ships have survived heavy coats of heavy oil. Swimmers who take on the English Channel encase themselves inside layer after layer of the thickest grease you can buy. And I have yet to learn of a dame dying in a bathtub— because her pores were "all sealed up." Even if you coat her face with Vaseline, she'll survive.

It's true that we must all eliminate sweat metabolites (proteins, acids, urates); and a victim who is totally varnished or really shellacked will get mighty sick. But it will take hours and hours and hours—twenty-four, say —of total impermeability before the hapless subject would be inclined to kick the bucket.

The disenchanting truth is that if you want to suffocate someone, you had better do it right: by sealing off (1) nose and (2) mouth. If you do that, you don't need to "seal up the pores."

10. Blue balls.

Suppose you are driving through the back country of Iraq one fine spring day, tra-la-la-la and all that. And suppose you see (as you will) that the sweet faces of calves are purplish in color, and all little chicks are green, cows' udders are flaming red, and bulls' balls are dazzling blue. No doubt of it: That's what you'll see in the back country of Iraq any fine day in early spring.

You would blink, of course, and wipe your sunglasses, and look again, and again, and swear off the hard stuff— but the astonishing colors would not disappear. Imagine what you would imagine: an entirely new, exotic animal kingdom.

That would be rash. You'd be better off hailing the first passing Iraqi to ask, "Excuse me, Jack, but am I seeing things or are those little chicks really green, and those cow's udders red, and those bull's—er—genitals blue?"

You would soon learn that few passing Iraqis understand English.

O.K. Take it from the top. Let's assume that the barefooted native in a nightshirt who is shuffling down the road is a graduate of Oxford, which is full of Rhodes scholars, and understood every word you uddered.

What he would reply, to change your dream life forever, is something like this: "*Ragoul* (man!), your vision, Allah be praised, leaves nothing to be desired. But your ignorance, by the beard of the Prophet, is scandalous. Surely you have heard of the evil spirits who can ruin an animal's fertility and demoralize its fornication? Well, *achi* (brother), those ancient, fearful gods must be scammed, or even snake-oiled. The way our peasants have done that for centuries is to diddle the dastardly demons each spring, when Nature's supernal cycle starts once more (praise Allah, from whom all wonders flow), by painting their precious livestock in colors dictated by tradition and proved one-hundred-percent effective; magenta for little calves' faces, green for little chicks, red for cows, but green for their teats. . . . What? You had not noticed?! The *cows* are painted red, Yank, but the teats are shiny green. Our crowning achievement is the balls of our bulls, which are concealed within blue as blue as the Mosque in Istanbul."

If you happen to accost an Iraqi chauvinist he will go on to remind you that you are standing on the historic ground of what was once Mesopotamia; that between the Tigris and the Euphrates stood proud Ur, funky Nineveh, swinging Babylon; that it is not uncommon for the alluvial plains to fry in 120° in shade in the summer —and hit teeth-freezing frost in the winter; that the effulgent Sumerian culture flourished here almost 5000 years ago; that Iraq and Iran are not only different nations but testy enemies; that Iraq has long chivvied its Kurds for their ways; that 74 percent of the population speaks Arabic and 20 percent Kurdish; and that the capital, famed in lore and legend, is none other than Baghdad, whose most spendid Caliph (in Arabic, *Khalifah* or "successor" to Mohammed) was one of my earliest idols, Haroun-al-Raschid ("Aaron the Righteous"), who is immortalized by Scheherazade in the best chapters of *The Thousand and One Nights*.

Ah, sweet mystery of Iraq! Blue moons, red cows, blue skies, blue songs, Iraq 'n' roll, green chicks, blue gowns, green teats, blue jokes, magenta calves, blue dawns, bluenoses, blue belles—and bulls blue about their balls. All brought to you in living, breathing Technicolor!

11. Flying saucers.

I am one of those lucky *Luftmenschen* who actually, unquestionably saw a flying saucer. Our plane was flying from Los Angeles to Denver when I spied the spinning dish—at 1:34 P.M. The saucer was an orange-tinted disk, whirling in a bright white cloud about three or four miles away. It was—oh, say, five to six inches in diameter, at that distance. I guessed it to be—well, maybe thirty feet in diameter, if you were close up. It looked like a small, fuzzy, orangy planet, with a shimmering flat brim, something like Saturn and its ring.

I watched the fantastic object, absolutely transfixed, then nudged the little old lady next to me. In as blasé a tone as I could manage in such mirific circumstances, I murmured, "Ma'am, if you would care to glance out of the window—over there—you will see a flying saucer."

She gave me an uneasy look, for which I could hardly blame her.

"I mean it," I smiled. "Just lean forward."

She leaned forward suspiciously, looked out, gasped, lurched so far that her nose grazed my cheek, and turned whiter than her hair. "Oh, mi*god!*" she cried. "It *is!* A Flying Saucer! Call the stewardess! Tell the captain! Call the Air Force—"

But even as she chattered, the orange spinning disk passed through the distant cloud and changed, as it swam out of that misty agglutination, into a small, gleaming plane.

"Oh, fudge!" the little old lady cussed crossly, "I would have sworn— . . ."

"So," I sighed, "would I."

Now, there's no doubt whatsoever that she and I really had seen—what? The bright afternoon sunlight, striking a cloud through which a plane was moving. The plane's propellers had whipped mist and light together in a spinning frothy sphere to make the prettiest flying saucer you ever saw.

It taught me a lesson I've never forgotten. I hope this book will do the same for you.

6.
THESE, YOU WON'T BELIEVE— BUT SHOULD

"When I was a boy I was told
that anybody could become President;
now I'm beginning to believe it."

—*Clarence Darrow*

I was sending a raincoat to the cleaners one morning, and in one of the pockets I found an envelope on the back of which, in my handwriting, some moron had scribbled:

JULES DUMONT
Longest beard on record: 11 feet 11.7 inches!

Now why would any full-grown male outside of a booby hatch record such a piece of nonsense? It is barbarous. That some French fathead grew a pussful of fuzz almost twelve feet long might quicken the pulse of a barker at a Freak Show, or arouse the ire of the American Association of Hair-Braiders; but why would an out-and-out square like me want to stuff his head with such spinach?

Even worse, why would the beard of Jules Dumont send me off on a binge of research so relentless, intensive and absurd that I finally made the acquaintance of one Hans Staininger, who had a beard 8 feet 9 ¾ inches long? Obviously, Herr Staininger's facial foliage was shorter than Monsieur Dumont's—but the former could boast of a fate much more picturesque than ever visited the latter: Hans Staininger tripped over his beard, broke his neck and died; Dumont just kept stroking his chin armor until he peacefully left this unworthy world. How do I know about Staininger's *modus mori?* Because it is memorialized on his rococo tomb in Braunau, Austria, where the old geezer is sculpted with this braided beaver trailing considerably below his harlequin trousers. The Mayor of Braunau will be happy to verify this if you write him a nice letter.

Let's return to my flagellation. Why would an otherwise sane, clean-living American of my age stuff his mind with such bubblegum? Because he is hopelessly hooked on facts. Any facts. The outlandisher the better. I am, in fact, a fact junkie. Facts fascinate me. They mesmerize me. They nourish my soul. They pour rejuvenating juices into my blood. Just as some kookerinos get their kicks from matchbooks, blazer buttons or (for all I know) Assyrian dental floss, I just can't help collecting foolish facts. I simply dote on data.

I remember clapping my hands in glee when, at the age of eight, I learned that owls (order *Strigiformes*) can turn their heads around an arc of 270 degrees. Man! 270 degrees! Only 90 less than full circle! (Imagine a beard 11' 11.7" *long!*) I once jumped out of my chair in ecstasy when I discovered that the zebra finch will breed *all year long* if given a comfortable nest. I nearly swooned when I learned that a sign language for mutes was invented by Jacob Rodrigue Peraire. . . . Sometimes I feel like the character in *The Mikado* whose

> . . . taste exact,
> For faultless fact,
> Amounts to a disease.

My only complaint is that I go around with a treasury of trivia in my head but rarely find the moment *juste* for flashing samples around to astound anyone within earshot. I can't seem to steer conversations to the point where I can smile casually, "But Oecolampadius is not a rare orchid; Oecolampadius was a religious reformer from Basle," or "*No* houses are numbered 13 in France; French addresses run 11 ... 12 ...12½ ... 14."

Oh, I have tossed such stoppers into a Jet-Set cocktail party, now and then, but I could not help noticing how swiftly the quaffers increased the distance between themselves and me—usually with an expression fit for a swinger from Maxwell's Plum who had stumbled into a taffy-pull.

So I have walked around for years and years, a fact-pusher yearning for people hungry for knowledge to beg me for definitive answers to such questions as:

> "What famous playwright used the pen name Hermione Whittlebot?"
>
> or
>
> "If all the progeny of one pair of houseflies were to live and breed, and their offspring did the same, and *theirs* did, too, and this went on for one year, how large would the total be?"
>
> or even
>
> "Are violin and cello strings made of catgut?!"*

---

* The answers, by the beard of the Prophet, are:

(1) Noel Coward; (2) The total number of flies, packed into one tight mass, would be over 95,000,000 miles in diameter; (3) No. The strings on stringed instruments are made from sheep, not cat, intestines.

Can you blame me for feeling like Victor Borge's uncle, that neglected genius who kept discovering miraculous cures for which there are no diseases?

Well, I have learned to live with the shamefully uncurious. I just ask myself the questions and promptly supply the answers. Here are some questions I asked myself only this morning, and answered with scornful aplomb:

"Can you sneeze with your eyes open?"

Nope. Or, as they now say, "No way, man. No way."

"How many hairs are there in an average scalp?"

About 2400.

"How fast does hair grow?"

I am not about to regale you with "The Romance of Your Follicles," but human hair grows about $\frac{1}{72}$nd of an inch a day—during which twenty to sixty hairs fall out. That even happened to Ziegfeld's follicles.

"What famous composer used to conduct an orchestra using only one hand? Why?"

Tchaikovsky. With the other hand, he propped up his head.

Poor Peter Ilich became so pathologically depressed in his later years that he was terrified that at any moment his head would fall off. Strangest *idée fixe* I ever heard of, and I've heard some mind-crackers.

"The tunnels under New York's Hudson River and East River, marvels of modern engineering, always amaze me."

They always amaze me, too; but such were marvels of engineering back in the days of Nebuchadnezzar II, who died in 562 B.C. He built (I'm sure you remember) the "Hanging Gardens" of Babylon—a scrumptious palace with great terrace gardens.

He also built a tunnel, over half a mile in length, *under* the bed of the Euphrates River, connecting the palace with the majestic Temple of the Sun.

But I doubt that the tunnel ever boasted a rush hour to match those on the IRT.

"How many eyes does an insect have?"

Some species have 50,000 eyes—I mean, 50,000 eyes *each.*

"How did Moses get horns on his head?"

By mistake. A translator's mistake.

Moses is described in Genesis as coming down from Mount Sinai with rays of light shining from his head. The Hebrew word for such emanations is *karan.* But St. Jerome, who made a Latin translation of the Bible (the Vulgate edition) in the fourth century, mistook *karan* for *karen,* which means "horn."

That's how Moses got his horns. Star of David my heart.

"Do African natives tell their children the story of Snow White? Hansel and Gretel? Little Red Riding Hood?"

You certainly came to the right *mavin*. In Africa, the tale of Hansel and Gretel is often told to the kiddies, but with one memorable difference: the house of the bad, bad Witch is not made of cake, but of salt. Salt is much more highly prized, south of the Sahara, than cake.

Snow White's adventures are solemnly recounted in the once-dark continent, but in the vast regions where no one has ever seen snow, the heroine is sensibly called "Flower White."

As for Little Red Riding Hood, the kid doesn't get much of a play south of Suez, except in Communist countries, where red is the right color for hoods—and unsurpassed for hoodwinking.

"Why is the obelisk in Central Park called 'Cleopatra's Needle'?"

Because some flack with a flair for phrases got away with it.

There are *two* obelisks misnamed so picturesquely: the one in Central Park and the one on the Thames Embankment. And neither has the slightest connection with Cleopatra. The shafts could more properly be called Thotmes' Thimble, because they were erected by King Thotmes III, sometime around 1500 B.C., in Heliopolis.

The largest obelisk of all, which was put up in Karnak, is now in the Piazza del Popoli in Rome; but no Italian in his right mind would call it "Cleopatra's Needle."

When I asked one sardonic Roman what *he* called the obelisk he said, "Whistler's Father."

"Is it true that in Burma no one is deliberately awakened?"

Hooey. The Burmese can't wait to awaken you; what they won't do is wake anyone up *abruptly*. They think that the minute you fall asleep, your soul drifts off into the ether. So, waking someone up too fast may catch his or her soul floating around in the suburbs, without enough time to reenter his or her body. No decent Burmese could have so fearful a thing on his or her conscience. And all this "his or her"ing is a cowardly concession to the Women's Lib campaign against "mankind."

"When we don't understand something, we say 'It's Greek to me.' Okay: What does a Greek say?"

You're *pret*-ty smart to ask that.

When Greeks don't know what the hell you're talking about, they grumble, "Stop talking Chinese." This leads to the question: So what does a Chinese say? What a Chinese says is more eloquent than what a Greek says: "Your esteemed words are like a Buddha, twelve feet high, whose head and feet I fail to recognize."

As for the Malayalams of southwest India, they voice their discombobulation with a flowery "I do not perceive the dried ginger of it." Poles complain, "I am hearing a sermon in Turkish." Frenchmen say, "Pray stop speaking Hebrew." And Jews, who like nothing better than mincing words, dismiss foolish locutions with a crisp, "Stop knocking a teapot." As for the Kalyikas of Miami—but I dare not go into that.

"Where does the word 'pixy' come from?"

Sweden and Norway.

"Pixy" is also spelled "pisky" or "pyske." Both are earlier forms of the Scandinavian word for a little fairy, elf, brownie or leprechaun. That word comes from the Old Irish *luchorpan*, meaning a tiny body.

"If you remove all the blood vessels (arteries, veins, capillaries) from a man of average size, how long would they be?"

Placed end to end, they could reach 62,000 miles.

If you don't believe that (an authentic fact), check it for yourself.

"What is the farthest anyone was ever shot out of a cannon?"

According to the *Guinness Book of Records*, 155 feet. The circus performer, Victoria Zacchini, achieved a muzzle velocity of 140 miles per hour. The Guinness editors won my affection by going on to remark that when Miss Zacchini retires, the circus will have difficulty "finding another girl of the same caliber."

"Where, if you happen to meet a tiger in a jungle, would you holler, 'Hello, Grandpa'?"

In Indonesia! Savvy Indonesians think that tigers will tear you to shreds only if you address them by their right name: "Tiger." *That's* why Indonesians sing out, "Hello, Grandpa!" (Americans versed in jungle lore may cry "Hi there, Clara Plotnick!" or even "Greetings, William Howard Taft.")

According to the headwaiter at the Jakarta *Réstoran* on 43rd Street, the most popular name ploy in his native archipelago is "Hello, Grampa!" because that makes the tiger feel like a respected, beloved member of the family.

Never call an Indonesian tiger "Tiger" unless you want to feed him.

"Do you know of any other name taboos as strange as that one?"

Hundreds.

1. The Kirghiz, a Mongolian people in West Central Asia, not only forbid a wife to pronounce her husband's name—ever!—but any name that sounds remotely like it. Let's say you are a Kirghiz wetnurse married to a nomad named Max. (That's just an example.) By tribal taboo, you would have to call him Umberto. You wouldn't dare address him as Rex, say, or even Jack, because even though each of those is definitely not his name, it just sounds too close to Max. That max a lot of difference.

The spooks that haunt the Kirghiz are so alert and sensitive that they are quick to jump to false conclusions. One Kirghiz woman whose husband was named Muzhda let her guard down one night when they were making love, and called him "Moishe." Muzhda turned to yak curd before her very eyes.

2. In Australia, some tribes give a man *two* names, one

of which is never mentioned in public; it is known only to insiders. (The same is true of American husbands who travel a lot.)

3. In the Congo, one must be very careful not to utter the name of anyone who is out fishing. Certain Congolese think you put such a whammy on the named native that he won't catch anything but flies.

In my opinion, a good substitute name for anyone out fishing in the Congo is Izaak Walton. I doubt that any Congolese demon, however well-educated, ever heard of him.

4. Isis, goddess of the ancient Egyptians, put the kibosh on the subgod, Ra, by turning his saliva into a snake, which promptly sank its fangs into him. To escape death, Ra was forced to tell Isis his most secret name (he had many). That name, which no one knows to this day (I think it was George Raft), was what gave Isis supremacy over Ra once and for all. Today, Ra is praised only by cheerleaders at college football games.

5. Many American Indians considered their names an actual part of themselves. They were convinced that if anyone pronounced your name malevolently, your spirit would be gravely diminished. Either that, or your elbows would turn into *knishes*.

6. Rumpelstiltskin, who was a deformed dwarf, killed himself when the king's young bride discovered his name. I have never understood why our children fall for such *bobbe-mysehs*.

7. In Hungary, centuries ago, men tried to outwit ghoulish revenants, who were hovering all around them in search of human prey, by using horrid, therefore protective, names for their children. The idea seemed to be

that a bogey would give a wide berth to a child (punning aside) who is loudly called, say, "Leper," or "Pimples." The Chinese follow a similar custom to this day.

I have never been taken in by such fears, because the healthiest kid on Kedzie Avenue in Chicago, on which thoroughfare I lived for eleven years, was named Lipschitz.

"Is it true that in Persia sailors used to beat the sea with whips before setting forth in a boat?"

Yes, siree! Persian seamen always flailed the water with laths, whips, bats or branches before they shoved off from shore. The whacking was supposed to break the hostile spirit of the sea before it got out of hand.

I don't know whether Iranian sailors still engage in this punitive insurance, but I certainly hope so. There's not enough water-beating in this world, if you ask me, especially in government budgets. If Congress had spent more time out in canoes walloping the Potomac River, instead of on Capitol Hill passing money-down-the-drain legislation, we'd all be a lot better off.

"Where is Mississippi Bay?"

In Japan. After Commodore Perry anchored four vessels, including his flagship, the S.S. *Mississippi*, in lower Tokyo (then called Yedo) Bay, on July 8, 1853, the duly impressed Nipponese changed the name of the bay from Yedo to Mississippi. The four *s*'s are a cinch for Japanese to pronounce. Sibilants are their favorite sounds.

"What do mathematicians mean when they talk about 'perfect' numbers? Give an example."

I couldn't explain it *unless* I gave an example.

By a "perfect" number, mathematicians do not mean the number has a perfect shape or deserves A+ in deportment. A perfect number is a number whose factors add up to exactly the number itself—no more, no less. (Factors are the "dividers" by which a number can be exactly divided, without any fraction "left over.")

Example: Number 6. This is a perfect number because its factors—3, 2, 1—add up to 6.

Number 28 is a perfect number, too, because it is the sum of 1, 2, 4, 7, 14.

Another example is—uh—well, examples of perfect numbers are so goddamn rare I don't believe it. There are only four perfect numbers in the first million whole numbers! Even worse, there are only seven perfect numbers in the first *billion*. And you'd never guess what the eighth perfect number is. Hold your breath:

$$2,305,843,008,139,952,128$$

This exhausts not only me, but my familiarity with higher mathematics.

"What do you think is the ugliest of all living creatures?"

In my gallery of horrors, first prize easily goes to the Star-nosed Mole (*Condylura cristata*), a ghastly mound of ratty fur with huge claws, hideous feet, apparently no eyes (they are the size of a pin, buried in the engulfing hairiness), with a sickening snout which looks like two

The Power of Positive Nonsense

dozen roosters' combs crammed together. (This grisly shnozz is actually twenty-two feelers, encircling what could otherwise be a nose and mouth.) The head of this utterly loathsome creature resembles a Hieronymous Bosch nightmare of twenty-two turkeys being swallowed *en masse* by a decapitated beaver with a lizard's feet. Please don't dwell on it.

The Star-nosed Mole is certainly uglier than the Sungazer lizard, the horrifying marine Iguana, the icky Trunkfish of Indonesia, the repulsive fork-tongued Komodo Dragon, the gorgonian Gila Monster, or the nauseating Greater Leaf-nosed Bat: *that* monster has a square nose, ferocious incisors, and makes my skin crawl whenever I see a picture of it.

The Great Anteater (*Mymecophage tridactyla*) is almost as odious a critter: over four feet long, with a three-foot tail, weighing up to a hundred pounds, with a coarse, furry coat. Its snout is so long I can't stand it. As for the Three-toed Tamandua, whose tongue is a drooping whip: it looks like an abortion produced by the liaison between a schizophrenic seal and a leprous lemur. And as for the armadillo, that fake lizard with 104 tiny teeth, you can use its carapace as a spittoon for all I care.

I wish you had not triggered these disgusting images.

"How often do we dream?"

Dreams fill up a whopping part of our sleep—about one-fifth of the somnolence, which is pretty darn large if you remember that we spend a third of our time on earth snoozing. Usually, dreaming recurs every hour and a half. Some dreams last as long as forty-five minutes; others seem to last forty-five years.

The most pitiful people I know are those so cursed by insomnia that when they do manage to fall asleep they dream that they are awake and can't get to sleep. This is about as dreadful a state as anyone ever dreamed of. It reminds me of the object that haunted the philosopher Georg Christoph Lichtenberg (1742–1799): "a knife without a blade that has no handle."

"How many bones are there in the human body?"

At which point? Almost 65 percent of the human body is liquid. Adults usually have 206 bones, but babies have up to 300. Why the difference? Because as we mature, our bones fuse. We don't lose bones; we just redeploy them.

You might add 1 to the numbers above—because an extra rib is given to some of us. Men boast of this because three times as many males sport extra ribs as women do. I don't know why; neither did Adam, who lost his spare in a way every red-blooded man with an extra rib would love to have repeated.

"How many feathers are there on a Whistling Swan?"

The so-called Whistling Swan has no less than 25,215 (plus or minus, say, 6) feathers. Mind you, no dolt has ever come up to me bristling: "How many feathers are there on a Whistling Swan?" I just thought you'd like to know.

"What is Louis XIV of France most famous for?"

He's most famous for at least fifty things aside from the fact that he never took a bath (I mean a real, total, naked, full-length-in-a-tub bath). But that's the characteristic of Louis XIV that thrives in my memory.

"Where is it considered a rank breach of etiquette to carve your sister's name on a tree?"

New Brunswick, Canada. Next.

"Where, when taking leave of someone, do you cry 'Hooray!' instead of 'Good-bye,' 'So long,' or 'Sholem aleichem'?"

In Australia and New Zealand.

Mind you (and this is *very* important), the farewell "Hooray!" does not signify delight on either the part of hosts or guests. *This* "Hooray!" is a form of encouragement, the expressed hope that good fortune will favor host/guest after they split.

I happen to think the salutation really works, because I've never heard of a host or houseguest who didn't feel a lot better the minute either stopped being either.

"Is it true that in Sicily, each Easter, peasants go up to their roofs carrying dishes and chicken feathers— which they fling down to the ground with happy cries?"

I don't know about the happy cries, but a bellhop in Palermo swore by his patron saint that in the Sicilian village from which he came, the natives dashed up to their roofs during Easter and hurled dishes and chicken feathers to the ground like crazy. The bellhop, who was pushing seventy, said this was an ancient custom which brought good luck and high fertility to the household in the year ahead. He said the thrown dishes created such a racket that they scared away evil spirits.

When I asked him what the chicken feathers did, he went to the men's room.

"How often would a tossed coin come up heads—or tails—fifty times in a row?"

Wow! The Time-Life Books savant on statistics puts it bluntly: "... it would take a million men, tossing coins ten times a minute, forty hours a week (to hit fifty heads or tails in a row) once every nine centuries."

The most amazing thing about statistics, to me, is that they are utterly fearless.

"Is it true that the chirping of crickets accurately reports the temperature?"

The chirping of a Snowy Tree Cricket does. Count the chirps for exactly fifteen seconds, then add 40. If the cricket beeps twenty-eight times in fifteen seconds, your thermometer will register 68. That's what I'm told.

There's only one catch to this invaluable tip: no one but a veteran cricketeer can tell the difference between the stridulation of the Snowy Tree Cricket, a cricket on the hearth or dozens of other varieties—none of which can be relied upon to give you accurate weather news. But then, who—except the Snowy Tree Cricket—can?

"Why is England sometimes called 'perfidious Albion'?"

There are several explanations for England's peculiar sobriquet:

1. "Albion" may have been the Celtic name for Britain, perhaps because of the white (*albus* in Latin) cliffs of Dover.

2. One legend has it that a Roman named Albion was the first Christian to be martyred in England.

3. My own preference, based on nothing but a sweet tooth for the exotic, involves a king of Syria who had so commodious and fertile a harem that he sired no less than fifty daughters. The oldest was a lass named Albia. The potentate's fifty daughters are said to have married on the same night: each then murdered her husband. Whether the murders were *pre-* or *post-coitum triste* I have no way of knowing.

The fifty Syrian widows were promptly punished by their father, who hustled them aboard a decrepit ship and cast it adrift. The boat bobbed around the Mediterranean, passed through the Pillars of Hercules, and somehow ended up on an English beach.

The fifty homicidal ladies went ashore, married fifty natives and, so the yarn goes, lived happily ever after. The oldest wife, remember, was named Albia. Whether her character was perfidious, I can't say one way or another. But I would find it hard to fall asleep next to a wife like that.

"How does a grasshopper hear?"

You'll never believe it, but a grasshopper's "ears" are located in his knees.

These, You Won't Believe—But Should

"Why do Japanese scrolls and woodcuts show the Japanese of old with hideous black teeth?"

What was rotten in Japan, unlike Denmark, was not politics but teeth, evidently.

Well, did caries run rife in old Nippon? (I will not stoop to puns about a caries nation.) No. Actually, the Japanese had teeth no worse than other people's. What accounts for the scrolls and woodcuts is this: The Nipponese deliberately blackened their teeth every few days for cosmetic purposes. They used a powder with iron and tannic acid added to perform this dental duplicity in the Sun King's kingdom. Let not the seeing cause believing: The teeth were fine, albeit the style strikes us as unbeautifying. But then so does the Russian penchant for a mouthful of sparkling stainless steel. Or the filed teeth of certain primitive tribes.

"Did 'début' always mean a social event in which young ladies were introduced to Society?"

No, "début" came from *débuter*, which in French means "to take the first stroke"—in billiards. How unromantic. A débutante is only a gal taking her first move in a game. Love and courtship, in French and Italian society, were indubitably an elaborate, stylized game. Much more subtle, complex and fatal than billiards. Even snookers is a cinch compared with coquetry.

"In which Balkan tribe do parents paint their front gate blue whenever a daughter reaches marriageable age?"

It's not a Balkan tribe, but a perfectly respectable group of Americans: the Mennonites. They live in eastern Pennsylvania.

"What is Weigert's stain?"

Hematoxylin, a purple die, made from a logwood tree. It is used in the examination of brain and spinal-cord tissue. It was first so used by Carl Weigert, back in 1802.

Weigert realized that hematoxylin has the extraordinary property of shunning healthy tissue and staining unhealthy or diseased ditto. Remarkable. A priceless boon to diagnosis. Pronounced "Veigert." German "w"s are pronounced as "v"s. That's why Germans say "That's vhy." (Actually, they say "Zat's vhy," but let it pass or I'll never finish this book.)

"What does 'chop suey' actually mean?"

Chop suey is, of course, unknown in China. It was invented by Chinese cooks in the mining camps of the West.

Chop suey means "different things"—from the Mandarin *tsa sui*, a sort of free-wheeling stew.

"Is it true that insects are very strong—given their tiny size, etcetera?"

Insects are unbelievably strong, given their tiny size and etceteras. For example:

1. A big, strong man has 800 muscles, but a little old caterpillar has over 4000.
2. Some beetles can lift objects 850 times their own weight; that's like Kojak hoisting 170,000 pounds—and you surely don't believe he can do that. (He can't lift 17,000 pounds, or even 1700.)
3. Insects sneer at fatigue. A desert locust can fly for nine straight hours without a moment's rest.

4. Distances are no big deal to insects. A monarch butterfly stores enough fat in its hardly-obese body to travel 650 miles without stopping for lunch.

Among the etceteras, I give you a random thought: Insects don't talk, but they stridulate (scrape their wings, or rub one part of their body against another, or "drum" out or "fiddle" distinctive sounds or songs) with charm and eloquence.

I hope Women Libbers will understand if, just for historical reference, I quote Xenarchus, an ancient playwright:

> "Happy are the male cicadas' lives
> For they are blessed with voiceless wives."

I would *hate* that.

"Who is the most famous monster in fiction? Frankenstein or Dracula?"

You've got your monsters screwed up, a dangerous thing to do unless you're an incubus.

Frankenstein was the name of the student, in Mary Wollstonecraft Shelley's famous story, who *made* a monster out of corpses from graves and spare parts hanging around the dissecting room of his medical school.

What was the monster's name? He had no name. I have never forgiven Mary Wollstonecraft Shelley for this.

Dracula was an unemployed count in Transylvania who in the dark of night sucked blood from fair maidens by digging his fangish bicuspids into their throats as they slept in beauty through the night.

The stories, novel (by Bram Stoker), movies and play about Dracula are based on hoary legends swapped around the campfire by the goatherders of Mittel-Europa to this very day. The thirsty count was supposed to be a vampire: that is, a corpse who became reanimated by leaving his grave at night and sucking life-sustaining blood from sleeping victims. Some superstitious *paraszt* swore that Dracula was really a vampire bat. Who was the battier, Dracula or his detractors, I cannot decide. All I know is that the count was a no-goodnick who did not make a single contribution to hematology.

"How many grains of sand are there in all the seas?"

What child has not wondered how many blades of grass there are in the yard, or the front lawn, or in the whole wide world? Who among us has not watched the sand trickle between our fingers and wondered, "How many grains of sand are there in—" well, in anything from a sandbox to the Sahara.

The question has always titillated me. I have not been able to uncover any reliable estimates about the number of blades of grass in the world (or even in Knob Lick, Kentucky, which is loaded with the stuff), but I am happy to tell you that the director of the Goddard Institute for Space Studies, Dr. Robert Jastrow, quite matter-of-factly writes, in his *Red Giants and White Dwarfs*, that there are "a trillion trillion ... grains of sand in all the oceans of the earth."

Ordinarily, I would snicker on reading something as far-out as that (*I* happen to think there are one trillion trillion and 2360 grains of sand hanging around, even if you exclude those trapped in tennis shoes); but scientists perform so many out-of-the-world feats these days (one casually told me, over a wet martini, that an electron is one ten-trillionth of an inch in diameter) that from now on when a child asks me, "How many grains of sand are there in the whole, whole world?" I shall answer, with careless aplomb, "One trillion trillion 2360 in the oceans alone. . . . What else do you want to know?"

"What is the technical name for a fear of the number thirteen?"

Triskaidekaphobia. That's from the Greek *tri* (three), *kai* (meaning), *deka* (ten), *phobia* (fear). This bores me.

"Is the sea squid as vicious as the octopus?"

The sea squid is much more vicious than its cousin. Octopi *rarely* attack anything, despite the canards of sailors; but sea squids are among the most ferocious predators in the sea around us. (I assume you are reading this in a rowboat.)

Sea squids are silvery blue, have luminous eyes and tentacles, and—all in all—look like a bad dream by Salvador Dali. Why, some weigh over a ton, reach sixty feet in length, and boast tentacles fifty feet long! Small wonder that they are extremely strong and disgustingly voracious. They speed toward anything from a herring to a submarine with murderous intent.

If you ever ever go skin-diving and have to choose between facing an octopus or a sea squid, I beseech you to select the former and flee from the latter, which is not easy: the monster moves via jet-propulsion, taking in water that it shoots out near its head—to shoot backward through the water like a rocket.

If all these facts are hard to believe, consider the topper: in an extremity, a sea squid emits a brilliant flare that lights up the whole area around it: this astounds an enemy long enough for the squid to make a getaway backwards. I can't guarantee that that flare won't help the squid find you if you try to hide in the briny dark deep. As for sex, the squidess often eats her lover. *Feh!*

"Who was Lady Gough?"

A bastion of Victorian purity. Her *Book of Etiquette* warned its readers to scrutinize their shelves to make sure that books written by men were never next to books written by women—unless the authors were married.

Scout's honor.

"Where is it considered an insult to ask a farmer about his future crop?"

In Muslim lands. An American agronomist, sent to the Middle East to teach their farmers modern methods of agriculture, amiably asked an Egyptian, through an interpreter, what sort of crop yield he anticipated. The farmer became extremely agitated—then furious.

The American was flabbergasted. Why was the Egyptian insulted by so friendly a question?

The interpreter explained: Muslims believe that only God knows the future; hence, anyone who tries to foretell it is a lunatic. So when the American asked the Egyptian farmer to estimate his future yield, the latter thought that the former was treating the latter as an idiot. Hence the insult, hence the rage.

"Who invented the umbrella?"

The Chinese. (Who else?) They did it back in 1200 B.C. The clever domes swiftly became a symbol of royalty—and of wealth, high office or social status.

The kings of Siam used to adorn the magnificent salons in which they held official audience with no furniture whatsoever—just three luxurious umbrellas. One majestic ruler of what is now Thailand signed himself: "King of the White Elephants and Lord of Twenty-four Umbrellas." He was admired throughout the golden courts of the Orient, and I cherish his memory. (Or should I say my memory of him?)

In ancient Greece and Rome, on the other hand, only women used umbrellas, which were considered effeminate. I can understand why: It is hard to imagine Achilles seeking protection from the puny rain; and Caesar would certainly have been the target of sneers and contumely had he appeared in full armor and laurel wreath (which he used to conceal his baldness) beneath a cloth canopy.

For centuries, tribal potentates in Africa and Polynesia have emphasized their eminence by appearing under an umbrella, held over their regal heads by slaphappy lackeys. No other member of the clan was allowed to sport so prestigious a symbol of power.

The word "umbrella," incidentally, has a peculiar provenance. It comes from the old Italian *ombrella*, a colloquial variant for *umbra*, the Italian word for shade. In Europe, umbrellas were used as parasols ("against the sun") before someone was clever enough to perceive the obvious: they could be used as protection against rain, too. (Hence the French name for them, *parapluie*, the Spanish *paraguas*, the German *Regenshirm*, the Hebrew *schimschiyah*.) It's hard to believe that it took centuries before a genius severed the cords of habit that regarded umbrellas solely as shielders of the sun. But that's the story of the human race.

"Is it true that the ancient Romans, when solemnly swearing to tell the truth, held their testicles?"

Certe. Recognosce tandem mecum—oops.

Yes, it is true that the ancient Romans, when solemnly swearing to tell the truth, held their testicles. That is where the word "testimony" comes from. (What the ladies did in Roman courts, I dare not guess.)

You might remember that according to the Good Book, old Father Abraham asked a servant to "put thy hand under my thigh, and I will make thee swear by the Lord ... that thou shalt not take a wife for my son [Isaac] of the daughters of the Canaanites [but] go unto my country and to my kindred." (Genesis 24:2, 3).

Between the Hebrews and the Romans, we have been testifying (*sans* crotch-clutching) ever since.

"When and why did the use of italics begin?"

In 1501, the Aldine Press published a book in a typeface whose letters leaned. The book was dedicated to "*Italicus*"—i.e., Italian. This was shortened, inevitably, to "Italic."

It was fifty years before someone hit on the invaluable idea of using italics to indicate emphasis. *You heard me!*

"Can any animals throw their voices, like ventriloquists?"

One animal has that reputation. But it's absurd. The American coony, a rabbity dingus without a tail, whose skin is found in many not-too-expensive fur coats, is alleged to possess the rare capacity to outwit an enemy pursuer by "throwing" its voice in various and deceptive directions. It does not "throw" its voice, any more than human ventriloquists do.

The coony is canny, so as it flees its predators it heads for narrow ravines, where its bleatings (or whatever the hell sound it makes) bounce off the walls and bounce back and make echoes—and thus give pursuers or gullible observers the illusion that a block of coonies is all over the place.

Coney Island, which made millions via thrills and illusions (the Fun House) and legerdemain (the Shell Game), did not get its name from the coony.

"Who best keeps a secret: men, women, children?"

Research by fearless psychologists reveals that keeping a secret has nothing to do with gender, shmender, occupation, hormones, astigmatism or halitosis. The keeping of secrets, like its absolute opposite, compulsive blabbing, is closely correlated to order of birth. That is, the oldest child in a family is the one least likely to blab as an adult. The youngest kid is the one most likely to be a tattletale.

If you think about this for a moment, you will see why. The young love to run to their older siblings with a hot bit of gossip, for a secret is one of the very few things from which small fry can get attention or gratitude from older fry.

I find all this quite persuasive. Quidnuncery remains with younger offspring as they enter adulthood, when it comes to full flower—especially vis-à-vis adultery.

"Who 'invented' chewing gum?"

It wasn't one of the Wrigleys. It was, apparently, a simple soul named Semple (William). The historic event took place on December 27, 1869, and life has never been the same since.

I consider chewing gum a supreme contribution to gracious living: chewers talk less than they would if not chewing.

"What's the longest any human being has been able to stay under water—without an oxygen mask, artificial lungs, air lines, etc.?"

Make your own guess by checking one of the following:

2 min. 18 sec.
3 min. 26 sec.
4 min. 19 sec.
5 min. 31 sec.
6 min. 39 sec.

On March 15, 1969, one Robert Foster was clocked within the water of the swimming pool of the Bermuda Palms Hotel in San Rafael, California. He stayed under for a whopping 13 minutes and 42.5 seconds. There's no doubt about that.

But there is a catch. Mr. Foster, an electronics technician, had carefully hyperventilated his system with oxygen for thirty minutes before he submerged.

The *things* people do to attract attention, set a record—or beguile a reader.

"What is Jacobson's organ?"

Anything but a musical instrument. It is part of the olfactory equipment of most vertebrate creatures. It is a chemoreceptor, a physiological organ sensitive to the chemical stimuli that arise from food or other odors.

First described in detail back in 1811 by a Dane, Ludwig Levin Jacobson, the organ bears his name. Fair is fair.

"Why does a married woman of the Todas people of India have to have a lover?"

I don't know why, except that it's an old, deeply rooted custom. Among the Todas of India, women have up to six husbands—plus one lover.

More interesting: Todas brides are expected not to be virgins. If a bride is a virgin, the Todas believe, her mother's brother will come down with a dread disease and soon die. But Todas uncles can escape death by shaving off all the virgin bride's hair. Don't ask me "Why?" about that, either.

The lover of a married woman plays a key role in Todas funeral rituals. If a married woman has no lover and leaves this world in that deplorable state, the wise men of the village rush to appoint one.

As Comte said, "The dead govern the living."

"Why do ducks have flat beaks?"

So that they can shovel food out of the muddy bottoms of ponds and streams.

"What is 'The Wife-Hater's Bible'?"

A printing, in 1810, of the Holy Book, in which this historic misprint appeared in Luke 14:26:

> If any man come to me and hate not his father
> and mother . . . yea, and his own wife also. . . .

But the true text reads "life," not "wife."

Bible boo-boos are numerous: an Oxford edition of 1717 gave the chapter heading of Luke 20 as "The Parable of the Vinegar" instead of "The Parable of the Vineyard." That edition, naturally, is called "The Vinegar Bible." Even odder is "The Standing Fishes Bible," the one of 1806 in which the "fishers" of Ezekiel 47:10 suffered a dropped "r" to become "fishes," giving us the tantalizing image: "And it shall come to pass, that the fishes shall stand upon it."

"The Camel's Bible" (1823) has Rebekah rising with her "camels" instead of "damsels."

"The Fool's Bible" that appeared in Paris rendered Psalm 14:1 as: "The fool hath said in his heart there is a God." You can imagine how energetically every copy of *that* Bible was found and suppressed.

"The Lion's Bible" uses "lions" for "loins" (I Kings 8:19).

"The Murderer's Bible" makes Jude say "These are murderers" instead of "murmurers."

"The Judas Bible" of 1611 published Matthew 26:36 using "Judas" instead of Jesus.

I suppose there are forty more. Apart from typographical howlers, the Bibles have one thing in common: they are priceless.

"Where did Cupid come from?"

From Medieval English *cupidity*, a mean, greedy desire for wealth.

Oh, I know the name Cupid, the Roman god of love, comes from the Latin word for passion or desire (*cupiditas*), but philologists assure me that my opening statement has much to be said for it.

"What is 'Piso's justice'?"

Something technically justifiable, but morally not.

Piso, of the distinguished Roman family Calpurnius, once condemned a man to death for murder. Just as the culprit was to be executed, the supposedly dead man appeared. A Roman guard brought him to Piso, and Piso condemned all three to death: The condemned man, because he had been legally sentenced before the "dead" man appeared; the centurion, for having disobeyed the execution order; and the supposed victim—because he had caused two innocent men to be doomed to death. Some justice.

"Is it true that children absorb Einstein's ideas more easily than present-day adults do?"

When the ingenious Swiss psychologist Jean Piaget tested very small children on their comprehension of space and motion, he discovered that the kiddies were perfectly at home and at ease with Einstein's conceptualizations. They were not at all fazed by relativity. (They changed, I should guess, after they began to study arithmetic and geometry in the schools.)

"How many atoms are there in, say, a grain of salt?"

One grain of salt contains a trillion atoms: 1,000,000,-000,000.

Anyone who cracks, "That's saying a mouthful!" doesn't know the number of grains of salt it would take to fill the average mouth. It would take more zeros than you can possibly imagine, or than I can cram into these pages. Even if I could, I wouldn't; it would drive my proofreaders up the wall.

"Is it true that polar bears hibernate?"

No. Only the female really hibernates; the male is easily snapped out of it.

The more interesting fact, you nark, is that polar-bear cubs are born while their mamas are asleep. When she wakes up, the cubs are eight weeks old and gallivantin' around in frisky frolics.

You'd better check these facts with a polarologist. I'm only repeating what an Alaskan kibitzer told me.

"Who was the genius who discovered the exact length of a year?"

Hipparchus, who died in 145 B.C. He figured out the duration of the year to within twelve seconds of accuracy. That was over 2100 years ago.

"What do chromosomes do?"

Francis Crick, co-winner of the Nobel Prize, estimates that the chromosomes in one little fertilized human egg contain as much information as a thousand books—each book the size of an entire volume of the *Encyclopaedia Britannica*. This incredible storehouse and control center is jammed into an area one-millionth the size of the head of a pin.

And it is this concentrated "instruction" nucleus that "tells" the human fetus when to forget about gills, when to start forming toenails, what color to make the eyes, not to get bollixed up over the vermiform appendix. And this intricate, compressed concatenation of chromosomes creates a cerebral mechanism so prodigious, so complex, so magical and marvelous and unique, to me the greatest wonder in all nature, that it can probe the stardust around Sagittarius.

"Is it true that the penis of Napoleon is still preserved?"

Could be. In 1970, at a packed auction of Napoleoniana in the main hall of Christie's, in London, an object described in the catalogue as "a small, dried-up object" was put up for bids. The object was identified as Napoleon's penis.

No tycoon or Napoleonophile was willing to pay $40,000 for the historic relic, so it was "withdrawn" (I am quoting the auctioneer) and returned to its American owner. No one knows who he (or could it be she?) is.

"Who were the Janizaries?"

Ferocious warriors, the elite corps of the Ottoman army. Some were slaves, some war captives, some Christian boys forcibly removed from their homes. All were forced to take solemn vows of obedience—and celibacy, which must rank among the miracles of military art.

The Janizaries became an arrogant and undisciplined lot. They loved to give a sultan conniption fits by setting fire to Constantinople. (That would give me heartburn.) During the reign of Ahmed III, *par exemple*, fun-loving Janizaries burned Constantinople, in greater or lesser part, 140 times. I find that as hard to believe as you do, but go fight history.

Anyway, the Janizaries (or Janissaries) became a hereditary cadre with so much power and chutzpah that in 1826 Sultan Mahmud II decided to dispose of them. He did this in the forthright manner for which Turks and sultans were famed: His Spahis slaughtered the Janizaries, down to the last man, in their barracks. That done, Mahmud sensibly disbanded the Spahis. I think no Turk, Balkan, Sultan or sheik ever had to read Machiavelli.

P.S. Don't confuse those Spahis with Senegalese cavalry of the French army, who wear those dashing operatic costumes.

"What is a fighting cricket?"

Exactly what its name suggests. The Chinese have kept and trained crickets for their fighting prowess ever since the tenth century. The insects were carefully fed boiled chestnuts and blood-sated mosquitoes.

Before contesting crickets were put into the ring, their owners made them furious by scratching them with the whiskers of a hare. I trust you will not think I josh if I tell you that there were heavyweight, middleweight and lightweight divisions for the pugnacious stridulators. How were they weighed? On tiny scales, naturally. Oh, those Chinese!

The official records of cricket fighters' matches were as complete as our baseball scores; and like baseball, cricket pugilism became a national pastime. The total amounts bet on the fighters cannot be reliably known, of course, but it should make you whistle to hear that a famous champ in Canton, who clutched at immortality as "Genghis Khan," once won $95,000 in one gala Golden Gloves.

Such tournaments, by the way, were not only "seeded," as at Wimbledon, but the losing aspirants to the cricket crown were eliminated more than somewhat, as Damon Runyon used to say: In cricket fights, losers lost their lives.

All this, mind you, from an insect which is so beloved for its "song" that the Chinese, Japanese, Spaniards, Rhodesians (of the Mediterranean island, not the African nation), Portuguese, Greeks raised them very tenderly and kept them in beautiful cages. I have seen exquisite cricket cages, mostly made of bamboo but some cunningly crafted out of porcelain and, if I could believe my eyes, ivory.

"Is it true that the beautiful magnolia is named after Charlemagne, or Carolus Magnus?"

That is an outright lie! The magnolia has and had nothing *whatsoever* to do with Charlemagne (742–814), who was, despite his imperial clout, the son of Pepin the Short, who deposed Childeric III in 751—and Childeric, mind you, was the last of the Merovingian kings, whereas

Pepin was a Carolingian, who conquered the Lombards and gave the pope, at that time Stephen II, sovereignty over the exarchate of Ravenna, a grand beneficence, known to us as the Donation of Pepin.

Where was I? Ah. The magnolia. It was named in honor of Pierre Magnol, a botany professor at the University of Montpellier—the one in France, not Idaho; *that* Montpelier has no university and few magnolias.

"Is it true that African parents don't kiss their children? Why?"

Most African parents don't kiss children—theirs or anyone else's. Why? Because kissing is considered the prelude to fornication.

The late anthropologist Hortense Powdermaker reported how horrified African natives were, on first being shown a Hollywood movie, to see a father kiss his child; they assumed that the man was intent on incest and wanted to destroy the screen in their outrage.

"What color is the blood of octopuses?"

Octopuses (or even octopi) have blue blood. Literally. That's because their blood contains copper. Not even the loftiest royal family on earth can make this claim, because human blood contains iron but not copper.

"Who is the President of the American Fertility Society?"

Coy Lay (M.D.) is the president of the American Fertility Society. I will answer no inquiries about this whim of the fates.

These, You Won't Believe—But Should

"How did Columbus sign his name?"

Cristóbal Colón, a name which the sophisticated readers of this learned work no doubt instantly recognize as his name in Spanish.

Before that, in his native Italy, our Columbus was known as Cristoforo Colombo.

On October 12, 1492, the great seaman adopted so cryptic a signature that no one knew what it meant until almost 450 years later. He signed himself thusly:

.S.
.S. A S
X M Y
Y po FERENS

We now know that the symbols meant:

Lord
His Exalted, Lordship
Excellent, Magnificent, Illustrious
Christopher

The "Lord" was Columbus' version of Admiral, the "Exalted" designated his self-appointed status as Viceroy, and the next three grandiloquent adjectives were his embroidery on his status as the governor of the island (and subsequent islands) on which he had landed.

In all respects, Columbus was a far more remarkable man than most people realize.*

* My favorite analysis and celebration of him will be found in *People I Have Loved, Known, or Admired.*

"Does anyone know the meaning of the words that the mysterious hand wrote on the wall at Belshazzar's Feast: 'Mene, mene, tekel, upharsin'?"

You're darn tootin'. The words mean "He counted, counted, weighed, and they divided."

Daniel 5 tells the tale of the great banquet of Belshazzar, the Babylonian king, son of Nabonidus. After wine had been poured into the sacred vessels, all gold and silver, which had been lifted from the Temple (in Jerusalem), a hand—no more—materialized, and wrote these words on the wall: *Mene, mene, tekel, upharsin.*

You may remember that Belshazzar was so troubled by the hand and its written omen, which he did not understand, that he had Daniel brought before him to translate the puzzling words. To the Hebrew prophet that was a cinch: " '*Mene*' means God has numbered the days of your kingdom, '*Tekel*' that you have been weighed in the balance and founding wanting. '*Parsin*,' your kingdom is divided and given to the Medes and the Persians."

That night Belshazzar was murdered, and Darius, a Mede, seized his kingdom.

That's the story told in Daniel. But biblical scholars today maintain that Darius did not conquer Babylonia: Cyrus did, in 539 B.C. The king fled. His son, Belshazzar, perhaps was slain in the fighting—sporadic skirmishes, at best, since the royal city surrendered quite peacefully.

No, I don't think "Eenie, meanie, miney, mo" comes from "*Mene, mene, tekel, upharsin.*"

"What does 'jequirity' mean?"

I used to think jequirity is the legal term which describes the condition of being in that state of estrus for which jequirs are famed throughout the Indonesian archipelago. I was wrong, because there is no such creature as a jequir.

Jequirity is the name of an American Indian licorice, or a tropical climbing plant.

The beans of the jequirity plant, sometimes used in costume jewelry because of their red and black color, are poisonous. Very poisonous. In fact, they are so poisonous that if a grown man chews on only one bean—not all of the bean, mind you, just a respectable part—he will die quite rapidly. My imaginary jequirs were never so unfriendly.

"What's the most amazing story you ever heard about Red China?"

Red china doesn't go well with a pink tablecloth. . . . But that's a crack, not a story, so here's a pip:

At a meeting in Peking, between Mao Tse-tung and the premier of a country behind the Iron Curtain, Mao asked, "How many people are there in your country?"

"Eight million."

"My!" smiled Mao. "And what hotel are they staying at?"

Incidentally, there is no truth in the rumor that today all Chinese cats go "Mao, mao. . . ."

"What's the most startling national custom you ever heard of?"

The Romanian custom, observed every June 8: They tie the front paws of dogs to a trapeze and swing the trapeze (and the dogs) back and forth.

I don't know whether Romanians still do this and I can't figure out why they once did this. I sometimes bolt up in bed, shouting: "What makes Romanians tie dogs to a trapeze and swing them back and forth?"

I *suppose* the custom goes back to the historic day when the dogs failed to bark at invaders, as the dogs of ancient Rome failed to do in 390 B.C. It was the geese who saved Rome. Their frantic honking warned the Romans that besieging Gauls were making a stealthy night attack up the Capitoline Hill.

Should some Romanian *maven* chance to read these lines, please resolve my perplexity.

"What are 'Mother Carey's chickens'?"

They are not chickens at all, but sea birds, gray-white in color, web-footed and belonging to the albatross family. They can fly very great distances.

To seamen of yore, the appearance of the *mater cara* ("Dear Mother") showed that Mary had sent out her little "chickens" to hearten the sailors with the knowledge that a safe port was not far off. These birds were the original stormy petrels.

Why "petrel"? That's fascinating. "Petrel" is probably a diminutive of *petrillo*. And what does *petrillo* mean? Little Peter. And why the connection of the birds with the saint? That's the best part of the tale. The petrels can fly so close to the water, legs and feet extended, that they appear to be walking on the waves! That, of course, was Peter's miraculous achievement.

"Who gave rubber its name?"

Joseph Priestley, the English clergyman-chemist-scientist who, among other feats, discovered oxygen (which he called "dephlogisticated air"), the decomposition of ammonia through electricity, etc.

Mind you, it was Columbus who saw native West Indian children playing with gobs of a gummy sap from local trees. The gobs fascinated the Spanish sailors because they bounced (the gobs, not the sailors). Columbus took a few back to Europe along with several other novelties he had encountered: the hammock, tobacco....

Not until three hundred years later did Priestley name the gummy stuff "rubber." Why "rubber"? Because he discovered that the sticky stuff could erase—i.e., rub out—penciled marks.

I haven't the faintest notion of what rubber was called before Priestley baptized it. Maybe *shmutz*.

"Why are black cats supposed to bring bad luck?"

That depends on where you see them. In some countries, a black cat is regarded as a sign of *good* luck. Charles I was so fond of his black cat that when it died in 1684, he grieved, "Alas, my luck is gone." He was right. The next day, he was arrested and handed over to Parliament.

In Sumatra, whenever the natives yearn for rain they throw a black cat into a river. After it emerges, the women of the village splash the cat and themselves copiously with water.

In ancient Egypt, the legendary Bast, a black cat, was considered a goddess. During the reign of Shesonk, Bast was made official God of the Kingdom.

In England, black cats were usually linked to evil witches—except in parts of Yorkshire, where fishermen's wives believed that a black cat in the house insured the safety of their men at sea. In consequence, and following the sagacious precepts of Adam Smith, black cats were so highly prized and priced that catnappers went around selling their felines, stolen elsewhere, in England's fishing villages.

"Are Japanese baseball players as good as ours?"

The Japanese are baseball fans without peer, and their players are gazelles on the diamond. They field, run and throw with superlative grace. But—. I always wondered how a Japanese team would stack up in the American big leagues in a regular season, not just in exhibition tours of Nippon.

Well, we now have the definitive answer. Peerless Casey Stengel, after completing an extended *hajj* to Japan, was asked by a reporter what he thought of the Oriental ballplayers. Dr. Stengel replied, "They play pretty good—for guys with short fingers."

"When did the custom of wearing charm bracelets begin?"

Who knows? Charm tokens, amulets or magical incantations were supposed to ward off evil in every early civilization.

Incidentally, "charming" once meant "on the way to the torture chamber" in England. In France, *charme* meant an evil chant—like the song of the Lorelei. Only in time did "charming" change meaning. The butterfly of flattery came from the cocoon of fearful magic.

"How are prospective grooms appraised in Pakistan, Bosnia and Herzegovina?"

In Pakistan, a young groom-to-be must appear before his future in-laws, who roundly revile and berate him. Why? Because if the groom can take expert abuse, he is thought ready to enter holy matrimony—tough enough, that is, to take whatever billingsgate his beloved may hurl at him in the years ahead.

In Bosnia and Herzegovina, prospective grooms are lavishly dined and boozed up by the bride-to-be's family. The gal's mother and father, however, never say a word (not even "Yes," "No," "Maybe," or "Drop dead") to the anxious suitor.

How, then, does the palpitating lad know what the parents' verdict is? Quite clearly: After the feast and palaver about dowries-shmowries, coffee is served. If the coffee is sweet, the young man has been approved for the marital match-up. But if the coffee is bitter, the amorous swain realizes he has been given the heave-ho.

I am greatly relieved that this custom never reached our shores. Judging from the coffee I have been served in otherwise civilized homes, American suitors would be in a hell of a muddle.

"What is the origin of the word 'boudoir'?"

It's from the French *bouder*, which means to pout, to sulk. Boudoirs, in the days when knighthood was in flower, were the places in a house or castle to which females were sent to get over their petulance. Sometimes miffed coquettes stayed in the pouting room for hours, and sometimes for joust a minute.

"What is a 'hinny'?"

A hinny is a hybrid offspring of a female donkey and a male horse. (A mule is the product of a female horse and a male donkey.)

Hinnies are not as popular as mules, for reason I can't understand. After all, a hinny has great stamina, is long-lived, and trots well. A hinny looks more like a horse than a mule does. Hinnies are bred a lot in Ireland, but there's no law that will stop you from doing it in Missouri.

"I once heard that the human body is worth about ninety cents—the value of the chemicals which make us up."

Things have changed considerably: the value of the elements you are carrying around so carelessly has skyrocketed—not because of the chemicals, but because of the enzymes and nucleic acids. According to the chairman of the Monsanto Chemical Corp. (and if he doesn't know, who does?) the basic chemicals in your body are worth around ninety-nine cents, *but* the average mortal's skin encloses over a pound of enzymes and nucleic acids, so even the most shiftless of our fellows is worth about $800.99: ninety-nine cents for the chemicals, and $800 for a pound of nucleic acids and enzymes.

I am indebted to the stockholder of Monsanto who announced: "When I hit $1000, I'm taking my profit and selling out."

"What are some animals among the endangered species in Australia?"

The numbat, the bandicoot, and the hairy-nosed

quokka. No, I did *not* make up these names. Check them in *The Larousse Encyclopedia of Animal Life.*

"What was the first statement ever made over the radio by an American president?"

I assure you that I don't go around scowling and kicking tin cans as I torment myself wondering what were the first words ever uttered over radio by an American president. But ever since I learned, from a memoir by Alistair Cooke, that the answer to this idiotic question involves one of my favorite comedians, Calvin Coolidge, I have pressed it to my bosom.

The place: Glendale, California. The scene: The railroad station. The time: 1924.

Radio was new, radio sets were rare. President Coolidge had just made a political swing through the Western states and now was starting back to Washington. An eager-beaver radio announcer waited on the platform of the Glendale railroad station, a microphone clutched in his hand.

A brigade of local officials, political paladins and Secret Service men cleared the way for the Great Stone Face from Vermont.

At once the palpitating radio announcer throbbed into the mike: "And *now*, ladies and gentlemen, for a real 'first' in history, you will hear the voice of the President of the United States *over the radio!* ... Mr. President, please—may I ask you to tell this nationwide hook-up, just as you are about to board the train back to Washington: What message do you have for the American people?"

He tilted the microphone toward the pursed lips of Calvin Coolidge, who opened them long enough to say: "Good-bye."

They don't make presidents like that any more.

"In what country do you insult waitresses or cabdrivers if you give them a tip?"

New Zealand, and you can fly there in a matter of hours. They are so egalitarian down there that a terrible hassle broke out when a hotel in Auckland tried to add a 10 percent service charge to its bills. Gratuities are gratuitous in New Zealand.

"What type of rodent is a titmouse and is it bigger or smaller than an American mouse?"

Shame on you. A titmouse is no more a mouse than a Welsh rarebit is a rabbit. A titmouse is a bird—a small bird whose feathers are rather dull in color, like the chickadee, who belongs to the same family and should not be confused with the chickaree (the smallest of tree squirrels) nor with the Chickasaw, who are Muskhogean Indians in northern Mississippi. How I do it, I'll never know.

"Is it true that some Polynesian languages have no word for 'time' or 'future'?"

That's not all the words they have no word for.

My favorite conceptual transformation is found among the Quechua Indians of Peru, who use "past" where we use "future" and "future" where we use "past." The reasoning behind this is more sophisticated than schizophrenic; the Quechuans long ago figured out that since past events can be recalled and visualized, they lie "in front" of them, before their very eyes, hence are called "future"; but events yet to come, being neither known nor capable of envisaging, obviously lurk invisibly "behind" them, hence are called "past."

I hope you don't think I could make up something as marvelous as that.

I may retire to Peru: I'd have a long, rich "future"— and no past to speak of.

"How ancient a sport is skiing?"

How nice of you to be interested. I don't know about snowdrifts in the rest of the world, but in Switzerland skiing is a much younger invention than banking, goiters or yodeling. In fact, no Swiss set feet on twin runners until 1890.

The only way I can explain why it took the Swiss so long to ski is that their minds were so affected by making millions of cuckoo clocks that they thought "skis" were helpful only in crossword puzzles: the terminal syllable of many Russian names.

"Is it true that in Bali servants fall asleep the moment you order them to do something?"

Yes. The Balinese have such a horror of being told to do anything that the moment they are bossed they fall into a coma. (When frightened, they fall into a trance.)

I am not exaggerating when I tell you that if you say, "Bongo, please fetch my wife's hat from the back of the car," you will have a narcoleptic on your hands.

The Power of Positive Nonsense

How, then, can you get Bongo to perform the simple act of getting your wife's chapeau? This way, which deserves dramatization:

YOU: Bongo, I recall that our car has one seat in front and another in back, has it not?

BONGO: I share that recollection, master.

YOU: And is it not true that when my wife, your lovely mistress, left this morning, she was wearing a hat?

BONGO: Verily, I did observe that myself.

YOU: [laughing lightly] I remember certain occasions when she returned *without* her hat. Ha, ha, ha. Can you remember similar events?

BONGO: [laughing joyously] Ha, ha, ha, yes, many.

YOU: So, Bongo, your mistress did wear a hat when she left this morning, but was not wearing one when she returned. Could it be that she *left* that lovely hat on the back seat of the aforementioned car?

BONGO: My! That might be. I regard it as a distinct possibility.

YOU: Then, dear Bongo, assuming you are not otherwise engaged or unduly inconvenienced, perhaps you could drift out to the car and observe with your own ever-so-acute eyes whether the hat of the mistress is indeed on that back seat we just, and so pleasantly, discussed.

BONGO: An excellent suggestion, master, and worthy of attention.

YOU: And if you *do* observe the charming hat of the mistress on the back seat of the car, could you be so kind as to bring it into the house where, I assure you, both it and your admirable services will be hugely appreciated?

Baliphiles tell me that if you talk this way, the chances are even-Stephen that Bongo will not fall into a trance. If I had to go through such Polynesian protocol, I'd end up in a strait jacket instead of a coma. But then, I've never been to Bali.